YOU BE THE DIFFERENCE

CHALLENGING AFTER-SCHOOL PROGRAM
PROFESSIONALS TO LEAD WITH CONFIDENCE

ANTHONY J. DAVIS SR.

https://www.absolutelydetermined.com/

ISBN 979-8-9901914-0-2 (paperback)

ISBN 979-8-9901914-1-9 (epub)

ENDORSEMENTS

~

"If you are a leader of any program, department, organization, or division in afterschool, K-12, non-profit, higher education, in a corporate setting, or even an entrepreneur, then you must read this book. It is not just a book. No, this is a leadership playbook that calls you to action. A.D.'s words, experiences, and insight equips and empowers you with play after play in leadership development. What I appreciate the most is how authentically honest he is as he reveals his trials and errors, hardships, and victories.

It is concise, BUT impactful. A.D. takes you through pivotal life lessons and decisions that will ultimately determine the aptitude of your success. ANYONE in leadership or attempting to enhance your personal development and growth will benefit from doing this inner work. This book is a training within itself and is strategically aligned with lessons and challenges throughout each chapter. Do you want to be the difference, make a difference, effect change, inspire others, impact communities and families; then take this guide seriously, do the challenges, listen to the lessons, and begin to revamp the way you show up at your organization. You will learn your presence MATTERS. After reading this book, your mind, attitude, and existence will change. I challenge you to bring Anthony to your next leadership development. After all, he is now your coach."

Rowina Petion, *Director, TRIO SSS Palm Beach State College*

"This book is an incredible must-read, for anyone who has a heart for serving in after school programs or with a desire to lead youth in any capacity. But I will go a step further by saying that this is a phenomenal book on leadership. Anthony provides the reader with vivid examples using his own leadership successes and failures. But through the examples he shared, **"You Be The Difference,"** absolutely oozes with inspiration, and will consistently offer readers practical challenges, valuable lessons, and useful tools. I'm personally eager to put these things into application as not only someone who's devoted to serving the next generation, but also someone who wears a lot of different leadership hats. Read this book and you'll understand!"

Mike Davis, *Founder/Director of 1 Body Outreach, Area Representative of Central Florida Fellowship of Christian Athletes, Varsity Basketball Coach*

"You Be The Difference," is a must read for individuals who work with after school and/or out of school time programs. It provides invaluable information on improving program outcomes, building relationships with community partners, parents and data collection procedures. It's your "go-to" book for training leaders on organizational development, managing and sustaining after school programs. It starts with YOU!

Jone Williams, Educational Outreach Director for the Achievers Program.

"You Be The Difference," by Anthony Davis Sr. is a pivotal read for those seeking personal and professional transformation. In my role as an Executive Coach, I've encountered numerous resources on growth and success, but Anthony's book stands out with its practical, actionable guidance. He skillfully blends relatable stories with effective strategies, making complex concepts accessible and engaging. Particularly impactful is the section on self-awareness, a cornerstone of leadership and personal development. As someone dedicated to guiding others towards their highest potential, I wholeheartedly recommend this book. It's not just a read; it's a roadmap to making a significant impact in your life and the lives of others. Embrace its lessons and witness the difference."

Kendall Ficklin, Executive Coach and Advocate for Professional Growth

DEDICATION

~

In the sacred pages of this book, I humbly dedicate my work to the younger version of myself—a soul once shackled by fear, doubt, brokenness, arrogance, and insecurities. It is a dedication born from the realization that just as God spoke in Genesis 12:1-3, declaring, "I will make you into a great nation, and I will bless you; I will make your name great, and you will be a blessing..."

Through the ebb and flow of countless days and nights, I poured my essence into crafting unspoken words. From letters to poems, articles to speeches, sermons to the culmination of this book. Each expression is a testament to the journey of self-discovery—a profound exploration of my thoughts, ideas, vision, mission, pain, hurt, guilt, shame, defeats, success, victories, losses, achievements, and the invaluable lessons etched upon the canvas of my heart.

Gratitude flows from the depths of my being to the Almighty for granting me the understanding and patience to unearth the strength and courage needed to pen these pages. To you, dear reader, this is more than a collection of words; it is a tribute to the resilient leader within you. Do not let the trials of life bury your confidence. Instead, let this be a call to unearth it, to rediscover the relentless strength that resides within.

May this book serve as a spark, igniting inspiration and motivation for your relentless pursuit of growth. In the immortal words of Les Brown, 'It's Possible.' Yes, indeed, it is possible to live your dream—to (re)write, (re)create, (re)invent, lead, enhance, implement, improve, develop, and grow.

"Whatever you do, don't let the enemy rob you of the peace, purpose, and phenomenal life God has given you." Believe it with unwavering faith. Behave in alignment with your dreams. Become the embodiment of your aspirations. For this dedication, let it resonate—your journey is not defined by the challenges you face, but by the strength when you rise above them.

Remember, leadership is not about a title or a position. It's about influence, impact, and inspiring positive change. Regardless of your profession, calling, passion, or mission, you have a unique opportunity to shape the future of countless lives. Embrace the challenge, lead with confidence, and be the difference that transforms potential into greatness. Your commitment to excellence catalyzes growth, learning, and empowerment. Go forth with courage, integrity, and a relentless pursuit of making a lasting impact. You are not just leading; you are shaping destinies. You be the difference!

CONTENTS

INTRODUCTION

~

If you're reading this, chances are you are either an aspiring leader, someone who has recently stepped into a leadership position, or a seasoned leader looking to enhance your skills. You may be searching for solutions to ensure you take your after-school program in a positive direction. Or you've been in the field for a while, and the pressure of meeting benchmarks to retain funding, payroll, and motivating attendance has overwhelmed you. The list is endless.

This past year may even have you doubting your ability to make a difference. What would you say if I told you, **"Confident leaders are built ... not born"**?

Like so many athletes, I experienced success in football at the collegiate level, University of Central Florida, earning national male NCAA scholar-athlete of the year, but the call from the NFL never happened. Where does one go from there? Taking the Program Assistant job with the Boys & Girls Clubs, BGC, of Central Florida seemed to be the natural career start for me.

I am familiar with the consequences of poor leadership—abandoned at three years old, living in homeless shelters. However, I also experienced firsthand, the impact a confident leader can have in a child's life.

Drawn to help kids who look like me, share my upbringing, or live in underserved communities, I am determined to make a difference in the lives of youth and families by any means necessary. My mindset going into the first year in the after-school program field were soon tested, and I experienced a healthy dose of doubts.

The year was 2009. With preparation from Kimberly Howard, and the leadership of Andrew J. Kirkland, I was promoted from Program Assistant to Program Director in three months. This man was the epitome of a confident leader. You can imagine how I strived to impress him.

My first big job required me to create the Summer Binder for one-hundred-seventy-five kids and twenty staff members. I worked late into the night to complete the assignment. Pulling from my past, education, and work experience, I compiled activities and directives to cover a nine-week, eleven-and-a-half-hour-day program. After I submitted the binder to Andrew, his response was, "It's trash!"

What?

He proceeded to tell me how he expected me to get the work done, even if it took me all night. It would've helped if he'd provided a sample or given more insight on what he wanted. We were at the deadline, so I didn't question him further, but went back to the drawing board, reworking and adding to the original submission.

As afternoon turned to evening, my wife called. She drove forty-five minutes to bring me dinner and helped me brainstorm changes for the next submission.

I submitted the work and once again it was rejected.

My confidence took a beating. The athlete in me resolved to work harder, overcome my failure, and turn things around. That philosophy had led to many successes on the football field, so I didn't think to change tactics after Andrew continued to reject my binder.

By the fourth round of revisions, the building had closed, the students long gone, and I was still working.

It was after eleven o'clock at night when I submitted that last time. The binder was thick, filled with everything from field trips, staff assignments, and activities, including anything I thought they might do during any given hour of the day.

"Are you sure about this?" Andrew asked.

"I'm as sure as my name is Anthony Davis sure." The words shot from my lips. "I'm done."

"I never opened what you submitted," Andrew said, without a hint of remorse.

I straightened. He had my full attention.

"I rejected the binder because you never fought back. You seemed timid and took my word as golden. Although I got a little more from you each time, you never stood your ground. Never claimed it was your best work. You lacked confidence when you must believe." I recall his words as if he said them yesterday.

That moment not only served as the first big lesson in me becoming a confident leader, but also the most memorable. I laugh now, but I wasn't laughing then. I'm sure I was as frustrated as you may be experiencing in your current leadership role.

Like Andrew hired me, someone hired you. That alone proves they saw something special and believed you were the one for the job, no matter your present struggles or doubts you may be going through.

Imagine my surprise when I learned Andrew was grooming me as his replacement. In his resignation letter, he recommended me, by name, as the new Club Director. Since then, I have won many awards for my achievements as a youth development professional.

Now, fourteen years later, I am the Regional Director of Operations, managing twenty after-school program facilities and I'm responsible for over 13,000 K-12 students, and 450 employees.

Andrew's challenge brought out the lion in me. I discovered how passionate I can become when I believe in something. Seeing how the trajectory of my career changed for having unleashed the power of belief, I can't help but want the same outcome for every after-school professional.

We will focus on after-school programs in general, using my BGC experience and stories to solidify my points and strategies to becoming a confident leader. It is my desire you let this book serve as a handy guide anytime doubts hinder your ability to lead effectively. If you are a newly promoted leader, allow me to be your Andrew over the next eight chapters, challenging you to develop your leadership skills by committing to this 5-components framework for building a confident leader:

- **Study to be SELF-AWARE**

- **Practice to COMMUNICATE with INFLUENCE**

- **Face conflict with COURAGE**

- **Live by INTEGRITY: MISSION, VALUES, and PURPOSE**

- **Build your team with GRATITUDE**

I feel it is my duty to empower, as well as challenge you—my fellow peers working in youth development—to believe in your ability to become a confident leader. You can positively impact a child's future. A child who looks like you, shares your upbringing, and lives in an underserved community. A remarkable student, whom I mentored after school through the BGC of Central Florida, blossomed into a trailblazing first-generation college graduate, embodying the transformative power of perseverance and education.

Do I have your attention?

Let's go!

STUDY TO BE SELF-AWARE

YOUR IDENTITY IS YOUR SUPERPOWER

*W*ho are you?

A confident leader's capacity to influence and inspire is rooted in their ability to be authentic. First, with themselves. Then, with others. People are drawn to leaders who communicate vulnerability, understand their own strengths, and acknowledge their weaknesses, welcoming help from other team members to offset their blind spots. This allows room to build trust with those you serve and adds credibility to your leadership.

In case you skipped the introduction, my career in the youth development field, specializing in after-school programs started my senior year of college, working as a Program Assistant, while I waited for the NFL's call. A part of me knew my calling was to work with youth, and I had planned to use sports to do it.

I reported to the after-school program every day, but my heart was still with football. Even during my employment interview, I made sure they were aware that if I received the call, my plans were to sign the contract to play ball.

They hired me. And because the old facility had a grass pasture, I was allowed to run routes each day as long as I fulfilled my duties.

My daily attire as a PA, consisted of shorts, sweats, and hoodies befitting an accomplished athlete, personified by trending sneakers. Even after my promotion to Program Director, my attire remained the same. And when I did wear slacks, I was known to have a pair of basketball shorts beneath, always ready for the opportunity to practice. But Club Director, Andrew J. Kirkland, wore dress shoes.

I'd often pick at him. "Don't your feet hurt. You need a pair of Jordan's."

Andrew wasn't moved by my words. The six-foot, one-inch, thin-framed man would never be mistaken for a sports fan. He wore his dress shoes *every day*. Not the same pair, but the color—always brown. They made it easy to spot him in a crowd, sporting a Polo shirt matched with slacks. His attire testified more to his relevance than style. He understood who he was, his assignment, and everything required to fulfill his roles and responsibilities. Better than any words he could have spoken in response to my jeering, Andrew schooled me by doing his job and getting results. The kids and staff respected him.

As you probably guessed, it was on the grass field during the forty-five-minute breaks, I found my purpose again. While running routes, the kids consistently gathered. "Mr. A.D.," they called me. "Can we join you?" I not only coached but used the moment to train them. Guiding youth was something I had been doing since my Junior and Senior year at

Boynton Beach Community High School as an Ambassador. In those early years, I visited elementary campuses reading to the students, encouraging them to grow, learn, and follow their dreams. Although I suffered the pain of hopes denied, I could still help students that may share my childhood struggles.

I soon learned, working with the Boys & Girls Clubs organization was not only a job, but the path to my true calling. With everything I had experienced, I was created to:

"Empower youth and young professionals to find courage and confidence so they can build their character to be a champion in life."

LESSON: Before you open your mouth, your clothes are doing the talking. For youth, staff, and parents to see you as the leader, it is important that your sense of self and style is easily distinguishable. Your appearance should make a statement about your expertise and professionalism. A clear identity will set the tone for expectations while creating a standard of excellence for everyone in your care. And like a team's or company's uniform, plans change. But take advantage of the opportunities before you.

The moment I took ownership of my new career direction, the Jordan's were retired. Andrew would probably laugh if he saw my closet today. Like a swimmer would never use a football players' helmet to secure their hair and expect to win a race, I traded my cleats, shoulder pads, and helmet for suits, Polo shirts, slacks, and dress shoes.

My duties take me into the classrooms, gyms, boardrooms, and onto the stage. Sometimes, all in one day. The casual but professional look lets me adjust quickly to change. I made the conscious decision to adopt an appearance that embodies the selflessness, sacrifice, and service it takes to successfully fulfill the roles and responsibilities entrusted to me as an after-school professional caring for and leading the children in the community.

Directors manage diverse responsibilities. It's a delicate balancing act. Generally, all after-school program leaders' roles may encompass:

• Caring for the well-being of all individuals.

• Hiring and retaining qualified, diverse staff.

• Having a solid plan.

• Fundraising (generate funds)

• Understanding child development and best practices.

• Establishing collaborative relationships with families and program stakeholders.

• Promoting and marketing the after-school programs.

• Remaining calm under pressure.

• Solving or preventing issues.

• Assisting in the classrooms, the outside space, or the gym when needed.

Beyond dressing the part, a confident leader must examine what value(s) they bring to the table. Take a minute to consider how your unique identity superpower benefits your work location. Does the program's purpose present an opportunity for your genius to contribute to the world? Which of the statements below best represent your highest priority?

• To always provide a positive and safe environment for children. (Emotionally, physically, mentally, spiritually, and psychologically).

• To give kids a sense of belonging, usefulness, and importance.

• To enhance children's self-concept, academic performance, and social skills as they learn to get along.

• Ensure children have a childhood full of play, adventure, and exploration.

• To create a community where adults and children experience a sense of connection and new possibilities for making the world a better place.

• _____

(Add your own words here...)

Complete the following genius statement:

"I am very passionate about opportunities where I get to_____. I go about it in a very _____ and _____ way."

(If you need help filling in the blanks, go to Chapter 8, the Toolbox, and use the website information to book an appointment.)

I have found Dr. Martin Luther King Jr. to be authentic. His transparency regarding his beliefs and vision for equality to be won through nonviolence inspired a nation to come together and stand for what they believed, opening doors to freedoms we enjoy today. This kind of authenticity requires the ability to fill in the above blanks accurately. But know that kind of genuineness comes at a price—be it money, time, labor, and for him—his very life.

In the words of Dr. King, "If a man has not found something worth dying for, he is not fit to live." Never underestimate the power of belief.

As much as I admire him and the work he accomplished, without knowing the man personally but based on recorded observations, we're totally different. Where he was noted to be a driving force when speaking on stage, I prefer a more conservative approach. His passionate words are still quoted to this day, where I tend to use very few words, or even silence, in conflict resolution. While he was a great man, we all must learn to be authentically who we are.

I tend to provide an upset parent with an empathetic ear to their problem or concern, leaving the speeches for when I take the stage. And even then, I'm not the great orator he was. However, I pride myself on my 98% conversion rate. That's me. 98% of all issues, even fires, no matter what it is, or how chaotic, they do not hit my CEO's desk. And I've been told I can be very effective in a staff meeting.

CHALLENGE: Be encouraged by great leaders, learn from them, but walk in your own confidence. While it's a temptation to clone the leaders we respect, it's important to be true to your leadership identity even in the infancy stages. Dr. King had a solid foundation as a child despite growing up during segregation. Overcoming trials and errors made the testament of his works so great and now it's time we overcome them for ourselves.

In the course of YOU becoming the difference, the journey starts with self-actualization. It's the reason I left the line blank above, for you to write the priority statement in your own words. Take ownership and do the work entrusted to you in a way that is authentic to your unique gifts and talents. Remember, it comes at a price.

I invested my own money to attend conferences, hired personal development coaches, and obtained certification to facilitate Kendall Ficklin's Welcome 2 the Jungle® personal, professional, and leadership development training, highlighting the four basic personalities that people exhibit:

• How they think and why they think that way

• Why they behave the way they do

• How they are best communicated with

• How they respond to unfavorable circumstances

Eventually, I learned to answer my genius statement:

"I am passionate about opportunities where I get to **lead the team by empathizing with the needs of others.** I go about it in a very **steady, consistent, and orderly way."** Realizing your dreams, being true to yourself, and achieving inner peace will determine how others view and treat you.

The year was 2021. The knowledge I acquired was put to the test. I was the Area Director in Belle Glade, Florida, managing the operations of seven facilities. We had a change in leadership at a particular facility—a large program, not under my care. My supervisor asked, or rather, volun-told me to hold the fort down until someone could be hired, making me the interim Club Director, all while upholding the organization's priorities, mission, and values as the Area Director.

The facilities are at opposite ends of the county and required me to commute over thirty miles away from the actual work locations I was responsible for, daily.

Do you recall the ten general roles and responsibilities for an after-school director bulleted earlier in this chapter? In addition to the added duties, there were fires the previous director had left burning, needing to be put out. Some staff were out on maternity leave. The board of directors was new. Parent issues were a problem. I had a choice. Complain about the workload or be the man of caliber my supervisor's request suggested I was. This was my opportunity to build trust with the organization I served and add credibility to my role as a leader.

Can you relate to feeling overwhelmed with no room to show the signs of fatigue professionally? Have you ever been in a situation that demanded most of your time, not allowing you to do anything beyond the basic demands of a day—being pulled in different directions. You've become the solution for everyone's problems and spend more time reacting to the current situation rather than accessing, adapting, and creating new ways of being? But know this, it's in moments of tremendous struggle that confident leaders are built. I had to focus on the bullet points that were most important, while juggling the remaining tasks to make sure they were executed on a daily basis. Being one of the greats, is a decision away.

Considering the hardships of my upbringing, I had to tap into my superpower to empathize with the needs of others. It was time to take ownership—like a quarterback given the play, he runs the ball, cognizant of the other positions while moving the team down the field into the red zone. Scoring in this situation would be for me to prioritize "providing a positive and safe environment for children at all times." I believed this purpose was worth dying for and made it my top priority. The rest fell into place, with the help of others.

In a very steady, consistent, and orderly way, I communicated the kids' needs to staff and fellow co-workers. Being vulnerable, I expressed my need for their help and unique expertise to make up for my blind spots in an area outside of my reach. An area in which I hadn't had time to build relationships. The staff filled the gaps and reached out to the parents, and community leaders they knew, who would help us inspire growth despite our circumstances.

Together, by the grace of God, we got the job done. And grow, we did.

It came at a cost of time, labor, money, and dying to self.

LESSON: You don't have to feel confident to take ownership of the opportunities you're given to make an impact and serve the needs of others. It's more important to acknowledge your blind spots, identify great leadership qualities in your team members, and respect the work they do by asking for their help.

Again, I ask. As a leader of your program, who are you?

What sets your leadership apart from everyone with a similar or exact after-school program? Your answers to these questions comprise your leadership identity.

CHALLENGE: Be authentically you—true to you, then others.

"If leaders make all the decisions alone, they're not leading; they're dictating."
~ Dr. Arnekua Jackson

Are your words and actions congruent?

When becoming a confident leader, it is important to always demonstrate character qualities that inspire the vision and motivate follow-through to those in your circle of influence. Your effectiveness is linked to essential qualities that include:

• Honesty - Speaking the truth and being open about your thoughts and feelings.

• Integrity - Do what you say and live up to your promises.

• Respect - Treat others with kindness and consideration.

• Fair - Uphold policy that ensures everyone receives an unbiased chance and is treated equally.

• Effective Communication - Be thorough, consistent, and straightforward, both verbally and in written form.

• Handling Criticism - Regardless of title, position, or level of compensation, no one is perfect. There is always room for growth. Receiving constructive feedback, either from staff or upper management, shows you respect the views of those who follow and support you.

I recall a time when Shundra Dowers, Principal at Glade View Elementary, gave me honest feedback on how we could increase our enrollment. The fact that she knew to address me indicated our program had *effectively communicated* our vision to help the kids in the community.

She suggested that the Boys & Girls Clubs, as an after-school program, could benefit the school districts in a more effective way by offering services the school districts couldn't provide. It was moments like these where I felt my superpower— listening and not talking—benefited me most. It's the best way I know how to show the other person I *respect* them, their expertise, and I'm open to *constructive criticism*.

Since the school's focus was mostly educationally driven, largely to meet their funding benchmarks, she suggested our programs help the schools raise the student's grade point average by offering conflict resolution, disciplinary, behavioral, social, and emotional services. At the onset of the joint venture, they committed to chart results from the progress reports and semester grades; especially information proving the positive impact the program's support services had on increasing low-performing students' grades and behavioral rankings since enrollment. Because of this *fair* swapping of data with the school district, the after-school program had tangible proof to add to our grant applications and secure more funding.

After that discussion, we became "The Plug," and developed relationships with all local elementary, middle, and high schools to establish how to best motivate the students to perform. For instance, we enrolled all athletes in the after-school program. These same students gained access to our homework services, which increased eligibility and resulted in improved behavior—used our space for chess clubs, the violin program, basketball practice, things to offset and provide additional support. Able to exhibit a partnership that showed charted growth, we gained grant money to hire certified teachers as tutors to work with the students. Then, the parents of these students united and supported our efforts. It could be because, at no additional cost to these parents, their children received tutoring through their program membership because of the grants. This benefit alone alleviated barriers in getting the kind of help their children needed. It took *integrity* from both parties to make this work.

LESSON: When you demonstrate honesty, integrity, respect, fairness, and effective communication, and respond properly to constructive criticism, you show others you are a confident leader they can trust and respect.

Recently, I led a team of confident leaders who practiced these elements in their work, and we were awarded a $5M **21st Century Community Learning Centers** grant for our after-school program. I will talk about that later in the book, so keep reading.

CHALLENGE: Make character qualities a consistent part of your everyday practices.

"Leadership isn't about telling people where to go; it's about helping people on the journey."
- Jermaine Thomas

PRACTICE TO COMMUNICATE
WITH INFLUENCE

2

PRESENCE: DEFINE IT, DEVELOP IT, USE IT

A **confident leader** must be present—mentally, as well as physically—ready to excel every day.

How you start is generally how you finish. Assess your attitude each morning when you wake up. On the way to your work location, continue self-reflection at the wheel and again when you arrive. It is impossible to be mentally ready to lead your after-school program when you wait until the last minute to decide how you will communicate your influence effectively. Last-minute efforts cause you to become reactive instead of proactive, leaving you unable to establish systems your team can implement.

When I was promoted from Program Assistant to Program Director, I had not taken any time to mentally prepare for the roles and responsibilities associated with the new title. I assumed I would be ready to deal with the day-to-day needs as they presented themselves.

During the school year, students usually arrived at the facility by 2 o'clock. But this particular day, I had just finished eating lunch at 12:45 p.m. and kids were coming in the building. No teachers were scheduled, knocking us out of ratio. The kids had to sit in the gym for hours. Without sufficient coverage, we confined their movement to keep them safe. College students were my staff, so a call to come in early was not possible. And involving staff from another facility would have been unfair. You can only imagine the kids' complaining.

Andrew pulled me to the side. "Did you look at the school's annual calendar?"

I had to tell him the truth. "No."

This was a missed opportunity to be mentally prepared. I counted that day as a M.E., mental error. But all wasn't lost. Being present, I was still able to learn from my mistake and live to see another day. Even now, the experience helps me to empathize and encourage other leaders when they have to take an "L", a loss.

LESSON: Stay prepared. This means accepting the responsibility of being a professional, making decisions, and taking necessary actions to provide direction for others. In this instance, the school calendar came out the first week of July. Don't wait until the last minute or first day of school to start planning. You need preparation days with the school calendar to practice scenarios and have five to ten alternate plans so you can be ready for anything that might happen. When school doors are closed or the calendars dictate early closings for various reasons, have a plan in place for early arrivals, and obtaining the additional staff you may need to step in and help. And if you suffer a M.E., take courage, being present gives you an opportunity to fix things and learn from your mistakes.

What does your preparation routine look like to make sure you are present mentally and physically? If you don't have one, I strongly advise you to start working on getting one. Check out the Toolbox to review the general daily routine I have developed through trials, errors, and successes.

CHALLENGE: Be present! Don't allow a lack of preparedness to be the reason you miss out on opportunities or fail to reach your full potential. You'll never have to catch up if you discipline yourself to do what it takes to stay ahead today.

Here are a few tips:

• Start with visualization. See yourself as the impactful leader you are. Imagine yourself in various leadership scenarios—planning, working with others, and achieving your goals.

• Think about the qualities you want to embody as a leader. What values do you want to stand for? What do you bring to the table to empower others to follow you?

• Find a mentor or accountability partner (or group) and talk to them about your leadership aspirations. Brainstorm your goals with those you trust and who have your best interests at heart, as they can help solidify your vision and make it real.

• Act now, don't procrastinate. Being a confident leader is about making things happen. Start taking the necessary steps that will be healthy for your progression.

It is not always easy to transform into your leadership role, being present mentally and physically. But it is necessary. Adopting these practices daily, you'll eventually develop the skills and traits of every successful leader.

Greatness is upon you. Act like it.

"Great leaders don't have all the answers ... and they're not threatened by all the questions."
- Irene Rodriguez

What lasting perceptions have students formed about your leadership presence?

As a nonprofit and educational consultant, I visit all kinds of youth organizations, K-12 schools, colleges and universities, youth groups, and churches in the United States. Soon, around the world.

I've spent time at agencies where youth make steady progress, attending regularly. But there are agencies where youth struggle. In my experience, the performance of the students is affected by the strength of the program's leadership.

As a former Executive Club Director, I recall a day my presence had to be felt by a twelve-year-old member. The child barely sat down. Initially, I made a joke, thinking the student practiced wall squats. But being mentally present in addition to my physical presence, I did not stop at an assumption, but took proactive steps to investigate further, to avoid a reactive situation.

I debriefed peers, staff, and interviewed the member's sibling. Come to find out, the child could not physically use the chair due to physical abuse suffered the night before by a parent. The student had been spanked so badly they could not sit down.

I went into protective mode before the Department of Children & Families, DCF, could get involved. When the parent arrived to pick up the children, I advised, "You're not taking them today." We waited for the sheriff's department to show up.

The eight-year-old sibling approached me later to let me know the victim never would have said anything, and they were glad I had gotten involved.

LESSON: Never underestimate the power of what your presence means to a child. Your influence could save their life.

At the debrief with staff, I was told, "Mr. A.D., we probably would've caved to the pressure and released those kids. Your presence was felt and needed." Because this parent often became very belligerent, staff admitted to being intimidated.

Considering the youth and teenagers who attended our programs, predominantly Black or Hispanic, historically they often returned to their homes without strong male role models, I intentionally stand in the gap. Clearly, these kids lacked the guidance, leadership, and protective influence the father figure would usually provide. Never doubt the power of what your presence means.

CHALLENGE: You be the difference! Learn your students' perception of your leadership presence.

What do they see when they look at you? What do they hear when they listen to your voice? Understanding what your presence means to the youth you serve is essential before you can communicate that message with every word and action.

Your presence establishes you as a confident leader and demonstrates how you want to be seen by the students in your after-school and summer camp programs. It is an important part of your personal brand and can help you build trust and credibility with your students. When you understand your presence and its impact, you can use it to your advantage to create a learning environment where a kid can grow, learn, and develop.

"Staff appreciate candor, transparency, and vulnerability from their leaders. And they don't ever take that stuff for granted."
~ Mayra Gomez

What does your leadership presence communicate to your subordinates?

It is said a picture says a thousand words.

Your presence, the way you carry yourself, the way you interact with others, also communicates a word picture, whether you're conscious of it or not. It's the first thing people notice about you, which can significantly impact how they perceive your leadership. And how they respond. A leader is only as great as the people willing to follow.

Early in my career, people said I would talk, tell them what was on my mind, like it or not. You could see them brace when I came into the room, wearing a look that said, "Here he goes again." Their body language told me I needed to develop how I showed up.

LESSON: If I wanted them to listen to my vision with understanding, respect my leadership enough to follow my instruction, and be inspired into action, I had to add another level of skill to my communication banks.

Enter the room smiling. Your demeanor can communicate much about your attitude. If you come across as angry, confrontational, or unconcerned, those around you may feel they cannot approach you with problems or concerns. Practicing being present, I'm intentional about asking people how they are doing and waiting until I get a response. If their answer is one word or only surface deep, I ask another question and wait. This habit has led to more meaningful interactions.

I recall walking up on a staff member having a meltdown in the parking lot. People are overwhelmed personally and professionally. They need to know they can come to you. But that only happens when your people feel you care. Although the career field of youth development is vitally needed in our communities, there is no sugar coating how hard the work can be.

But I must warn you. There must be balance. If you're always smiling and friendly, those who work for you could misunderstand and assume you do not take the job seriously. It is important to strike a balance with your demeanor.

CHALLENGE: No matter your level of leadership, develop a demeanor that communicates you will bear the burdens of your peers and subordinates.

The following are a few body language actions you can practice and enhance your leadership demeanor:

• Upright and open posture: Confident leaders stand tall with their shoulders back and their chest open to convey self-assurance and an open mindedness.

• Balanced stance: Confident leaders demonstrate stability and composure when they distribute their weight evenly on both feet.

• A firm handshake: When greeting others, confident leaders offer a firm, but non-aggressive, handshake, indicating their assertiveness and control.

• Direct eye contact: Confident leaders maintain steady eye contact during conversations, showing engagement, attentiveness, and a sense of authority.

• Relaxed facial expression: Confident leaders avoid excessive frowning, furrowing of the brow, or other signs of tension.

• Engaged body language: Confident leaders lean slightly forward when listening to others, displaying active interest and involvement in the conversation.

• Minimize fidgeting: Confident leaders avoid fidgeting, excessive tapping, or other nervous habits that can convey uncertainty or lack of self-assurance.

Confident leaders know they cannot learn everything all at once. Identify one or two of the previous traits you need to work on and do so until it is engrained in your body language, then move on to others. Finding the right middle ground helps you lead others to the promised land. Operate in a healthy and conducive space and watch how your operation skyrocket!

"Excellent youth leaders are committed to these three things: supporting staff, connecting with kids, and building positive culture."
~ Dr. Derrick Hibler

How are you communicating your influence to the parents and guardians in your program?

I once held a workshop as the keynote speaker at a parent conference in Leon County, Florida. During the four-hour-drive from Orlando, I could not stop thinking of how important it was to convey our need for parents to continue involvement in their child's education even after their elementary years. Parents are the key to making a difference in the lives of their children.

Calling it like it is: "Too many students, especially in our communities in America, are underperforming in academics and socially because of a lack of parental involvement."

My presentation was a huge success because the parents were enthusiastically taking part in the call-to-action. I challenged them to find an accountability partner to hold their feet to the fire about being more actively involved in their child's development. It was nice to see them, from the time I walked into the facility, receive me, and respect the message. These parents saw me as a source of information. I strongly reiterated to them, "You are the number one determinant of the success of your children. You have power over their outcomes. Yes, that's what I said!" That's when a parent on the front row yelled back, "Say it again, Mr. Davis. Say it again for the people in the back!"

LESSON: To be truly present, a confident leader must not be afraid to speak truth with authority even when it hurts. How else will they know what to fix if they do not know what is broken?

When parents are working two and three jobs to care for three to four kids, they are not prioritizing sitting with a seventh grader who they believe knows how to do their homework. Keeping a roof over their heads, food in their stomach, and shoes on their ever-growing feet will supersede every time. It is our job to remind the parents/guardians and become their support to help their children.

CHALLENGE: It is incumbent on schools, community organizations, and agencies to create mechanisms to increase parental engagement. You and your staff should brainstorm ways to help the parents.

Here are a few ideas to get you started:

• Provide a list of free phone features that allow FaceTime on a break or between jobs for the parent to check in on a child to review homework, to check progress, or to simply lend an encouraging word.

• Provide a list of encouraging statements for the parents, known to motivate children.

• Provide a contact list the parent can use to get academic help when they are unable to answer a homework question, so they feel less intimidated to get involved at the higher levels of education.

• At pick up, ask if they need any help or if there are any present conflicts you can assist them with.

• Provide resources.

• And smile!

Youth development organizations and other community agencies must make themselves available to families to provide the necessary support for students to achieve excellence in and outside the classroom.

I encourage all after-school professionals to maximize your visibility and interactions during school hours and at school functions like back-to-school nights to build a strong leadership presence. Your demeanor is crucial because it sets the tone for your relationship with the parents/guardians of the students in your program. If you seem closed off or unapproachable, they may be less likely to talk to you about their child's participation in your program.

What does your leadership presence mean to your student's parents, then? How they see you will impact their engagement in their children's life.

In the end, it is important to be aware of your demeanor and ensure it sends the right message to the parents.

"Youth directors don't set the tone at staff meetings. They set the tone in the hallway, in the classrooms/program areas ... and with all the little conversations."
~ LaTricia Jenkins

How do you use your presence to benefit your after-school program?

The year was 2008. I was assigned to a facility known for "things going down," in a community ranked as the lowest economic city in the state.

An eighth-grade boy needed help with his math. Everyone talked about how they hadn't been able to get through to the young man. How he couldn't get it.

I had to quickly embody "whatever it takes." This was the same way I chose to show up on the field as a wide receiver. I'd run the routes no one wanted. Take the paths that required me to go across the middle. Give me the dirty work was my mindset. I'd do anything to set the team up to win.

I got on the student's level. Talked to him in a way he liked to be communicated to, and he got it.

It had always been my plan to take my NFL money and invest in a community center for kids. I never wanted a child to suffer the way I had. If not on the football field, my mind was made up to remain present and get these kids the help they needed. This child was just one example of those we have reached through this program.

LESSON: There is no such thing as "nothing can be done." When one door closes, another opens. In some situations, you must run with a "whatever it takes" attitude.

Like me, set your mind to give those hardcore, chaotic cases —the kids no one else can reach, the things no one gave you at their age, but you needed. To be the difference, you have to love the environment, the areas people deemed unredeemable. The tougher the case the better.

What can YOU do to reach the unreachable?

CHALLENGE: Don't accept someone else's results. Exhaust all your skills, influence, and resources to help your kids succeed.

"Managers stop by to make sure you're working. Leaders stop by to encourage you in your work."
~Ricky Hammond Sr.

FACE CONFLICT WITH COURAGE

3

IMPACT: INSPIRE, INNOVATE, IGNITE

*H*ow does your leadership influence your youth program's reputation?

Most people are familiar with the power of corporate branding. So much so, many consumers only shop certain stores or purchase specific products because they believe certain brands are superior.

For the athlete who wants to run fast, or across the country... it's the swoosh. If they want a hot cereal for breakfast to keep the hunger away all day, it's the quaker they trust. But if it's a quick, reliable, cup of coffee they want, they're pulling up to the golden arches for the brew in a yellow cup. Got to have a computer for creating content? The savvy consumer bites the apple no matter the expense. The brand people can trust to do what it says it will do—this kind of accumulation of perceptions is what you want for the organization you represent.

Parents are your customers and the kids the clients. There should be touch points with them even when there's nothing going on.

Make sure no one is a stranger. Speak to them at a game, in the pick-up line, for pizza, or a quick chat in the locker rooms to prove you're that brand who cares. Then, when you say something about Jimmy, the parents feel comfortable receiving the information—negative or positive—knowing you genuinely care.

When a parent sees you walk into a room, or appear at a school ceremony, does your organization come to mind in a positive light for them. Do they see themselves entrusting you and your organization with their child(ren's) care? Can the parents imagine themselves teaming up with you to ensure their child's future through academia?

LESSON: Meet them where they are and become the familiar brand, they know and trust to partner with to ensure their child's future. It's a hard sell to convince someone you don't know, to buy into your agency's services. However, pitching your ideas to someone you've spoken to at a game, in the office, or in the parking lot is a soft sell.

Does looking at yourself as a brand sound clinical, or maybe even cynical? Branding is no more than recognition of a person, place, or thing. You are the recognized face of your program. Once leadership develops good rapport with school principals, donors, the community, parents, and kids by following through on partnership offerings, a brand is built. We need to be able to sell our services with confidence. I'd hate for a leader's lack of branding to keep them from getting to all the people they could help.

The Junior staff program is probably our most branded service among the kids when they refer to what impacted them most at the Boys & Girls Clubs organization. For many, this program was their first time working. It gave teenagers (ages 15 to 18) an opportunity to find out who they were, how to identify their strengths and areas of growth, and it gave them a sense of belonging as well as responsibility.

Many earned a paycheck for the first time. For those like me at that age, they wanted to have a fresh pair of kicks for that first day of school. Especially, when they reach the age when the family says, "You can buy your own school clothes." I can still hear my grandma saying, *"Well, I'm gonna buy the Kmart clothes. If you want that ole Polo, and all the other name brands, you go buy that with your money."*

More than making them responsible, the exposure to work helped the kids decide what they wanted to do with their lives. I know because many have come back to pay homage, singing the praises of the program.

One of my best innovations to date, was organizing our parent committee CAB, Community Advisory Board. Our slogan was "Driving kids to success." I was blessed to cherry-pick parents and partner their strengths with the needs of the youth we served. I recall sharing with them how I wanted to have an award ceremony. I pictured serving food, giving awards, and celebrating all the achievements that should be recognized. They got excited.

One parent said, "My dad owns six Papa John's. I can get pizza."

My mind automatically went to tallying up the expenses. "How much will it cost?"

"Nothing." She cut me off before I could say more. "My children go here. Y'all have done enough. My dad will be okay."

Another parent chimed in. "I can get Wal-Mart gift cards." He was a general manager. "With what I've seen the last couple of years, as a result of your work in the community, the crime rate has dropped."

The hard work paid off. Parents came out of the woodwork to help with the ceremony. At the end, we were able to give "Thank You" plaques to the parents who participated with me behind the scenes. I'm happy to report that the next year more parents participated with CAB and gave back.

Questions to ask yourself: Does your organization's brand, or if you're a satellite location of a more prominent brand, inspire loyalty? How does your leadership influence your program's brand? Is your program's branding a representative of the culture, climate, and performance of your work location? Is your staff aware of the importance of your organization's branding? Is it you or your staff who helped shape the brand? Or did it evolve haphazardly without your involvement?

If you want your youth program to have a positive reputation, the brand must be important to the leader first. It starts with being clear about your goals, maintaining high standards, and always acting in the best interest of your team and the young people you serve. This foundation helps ensure that your organization is seen in a positive light by those on the outside.

CHALLENGE: Become the go-to after-school program whose branding is never confused with being the "babysitter," but the agency that genuinely makes a difference in the lives of young people.

Trust me, parents want to send their child(ren) to an after-care program that implements what leaders like Karen Pittman, Merita Irby, Thaddeus Ferber, and Dr. Richard

Lerner call "The 5C's of Positive Youth Development (now contains 6C's):

• Connection- A feeling of safety, structure, and belonging; positive bonds with people and social institutions.

• Confident- A sense of self-worth and mastery; having a belief in one's capacity to succeed.

• Competence- The ability to act effectively in school, in social situations, and at work.

• Character- Taking responsibility; a sense of independence and individuality; connection to principles and values.

• Contribution- Active participation and leadership in a variety of settings; making a difference.

• Caring- Sympathy and empathy for others; commitment to social justice.

Your leadership impacts your youth program's reputation in several ways. How you treat your staff, the quality of your programming, and your interactions with the community will shape how others see your program.

"Behind every successful after-school director is a staff team who are crushing it."
~ Carneisha Caple

How does your leadership impact the mission and vision?

Mission:

Ex. "To enable all young people, especially those who need us most, to reach their full potential as productive, caring, responsible citizens."

Vision:

Ex. "Provide a world-class program experience that assures success is within reach of every young person who enters our doors, with all members on track to graduate from high school with a plan for the future, demonstrating good character and citizenship, and living a healthy lifestyle."

Your organization's mission refers to "who we are and what values we provide," while the vision refers to "what we want to become."

Simply put, your organization's mission is its foundation. When a youth development agency is serious about its mission, everyone knows it. Even to the point of implementing a requirement for staff and sometimes the youth members to recite these worthy phrases daily. The basic standard is to display both statements throughout the work location, including every outdoor program area. Authentic leadership goes beyond posting the information but ensures every location "walks" in its mission, vision, and values daily. This includes youth academic performance, social-emotional growth, and plans for post-secondary graduation.

It's far more important that the program leader be aware of their personal decisions' and how their actions align with the organization's foundational beliefs. Once, I had to cover for an executive director who seemed to excel in every area of leadership. This staff member could recite the mission and vision statement on command.

The individual went on vacation, and I covered for him at the facility. A parent came in hot. "I want my receipt. We ain't got no field trip going on." She got louder with every word. "He told me he was gonna get me my receipt."

"All right, cool." I held her gaze. Nodding to let the mother know she had my full attention. When someone is stressed, you can't expect them to be calm under pressure. But once she settled, I called the director, and he emphatically stated he did not receive any field trip money from the mother.

Then she started name dropping. "That person was in the room when I gave him the money."

"I'll get to the bottom of this," I assured the mother. After she calmed, I asked for time to get answers.

I hunted down the names of the staff members she listed. They validated she had dropped off a cash payment.

When I contacted the accused director, that person lied until I asked for the bank statements. Then, there was the offer to transfer the money back into the after-school program's accounts and let things go back to normal.

Thankfully, we were able to reimburse the money and give the mother a receipt to match the original transaction without her asking for a refund. She could have publicized what happened.

Considering our funding is largely based on our ability to convey our integrity, this could've been bad. The parent was more concerned with making things right. She took me at my word and reputation that this was an isolated incident, the staff member would be reprimanded, and his actions were not the brand of our organization.

But because a confident leader embodies the mission and vision entrusted to them... Because a confident leader protects the integrity of the organization... Because a confident leader protects the interest of their customers and clients first... We let him go. Even though the decision meant more work for us.

"Anyone willing to take out of the mouths of kids, jeopardize the organization for two hundred dollars, or in the words of my uncle, '200 *funky* dollars,' you can keep that crap."

LESSON: Everything you do—from communicating with your team to allocating resources—can significantly impact your program or organization's mission and vision. When parents are angry, listen. Give them a timeframe in which you plan to address their concerns. Follow through.

If you want to be an outstanding youth development professional, you must correctly access, adjust, and take real action toward improving your conflict resolution skills. Not dealing with problems head-on can foster an unwanted culture or norm for your staff and students. Then there are times when our actions do not align and negatively impact the mission and vision. It is counterproductive to let mediocrity sink into your operation. I was guilty of all the above.

Once, I hired a close friend. A person I considered family. Together, we were winning. Our styles aligned and I believed I knew him very well. Then things changed.

According to other staff, he sabotaged my leadership efforts.

In disbelief, I delayed having *the* conversation. Everyone must have misunderstood. I would have started an investigation if it had been any other person. Bad judgement on my part, but you can see everything perfectly in hindsight. Even after I continued receiving reports about certain tasks he performed and behaviors exhibited, I could not see past the friendship that made everything all right. Because I did not deal with matters head-on, everything went south, quickly, and tension spread through the building.

Because I was so blinded, I acted unprofessionally. My first mistake was treating my friend as an equal when I was his supervisor, blurring the lines of respect. Because I was passive and ignored the warnings, others lost respect for my leadership, causing a rift in the facility.

I'm reserved and not combative, so my friend's negative attitude toward my leadership went unchallenged and garnered a lot of attention from co-workers who sided with him fueling a toxic environment. The situation escalated until I was forced to walk away from the organization. And the friendship ended.

Now, I avoid hiring friends. However, you also must realize friendships will develop with team members over time. Don't make the mistakes I did. Clearly communicate role responsibilities, expectations, and your authority with your staff often.

Believe it or not, you are the determining factor in changing your program environment, especially if it is hostile or toxic.

More thoughts for self- and program reflection: What does your leadership do for the organization or program's vision and mission? Are you strongly advocating for internalizing values related to those integral portions of your program? Are your youth agency's vision and mission well-known in the broader community? Are they driving the work of your facility? Do your vision and mission "walk" with staff and the youth you serve? Marinate on those questions.

CHALLENGE: Leaders, check your leaders. It's not enough to interview well, recite the mission and vision statement, or look the part. Character isn't something you buy at Walmart but is found in the integrity of the work.

"Leadership is not always about having all the answers ... or articulating bold visions. Sometimes it's just about providing relentless support to those in the trenches."
- Henry Saxon

How your leadership impacts the culture and climate of the after-school program.

When I became the Director of Operations at the Boys & Girls Clubs in Palm Beach County, I followed a quiet ritual every year. I'd go into the empty gymnasium the night before, during, and after our area graduation ceremony to witness the end results of choosing to be an active member. Lastly, I would sit with the seniors and reflect on the year that had passed and the ones ahead. Creating a culture and environment that inspires the young people you serve is crucial.

The first two nights I focused on whether our graduates had been provided with a supportive learning environment that would enable them to excel in the future. On the third night, I turned my attention to the new program members. I wanted to think about whether the facility's culture and climate were welcoming enough. Additionally, my thoughts concentrated on what adjustments might be needed during the summertime, in June, for the start of the next school year in mid-August. From that third night onward, I was obsessive about what our young people would experience during the first day of our summer, after-school programs, and beyond.

This ritual played a significant role in closing the school year, visualizing our summer camp, and building a bridge for the upcoming school year in the fall.

Please know, all I accomplished as the Director of Operations was possible because of the organization's incredible staff and community leaders in four cities in Florida: Belle Glade, Canal Point, Pahokee, and South Bay.

I was responsible for overseeing seven program locations in those cities, all within a 14-mile radius. I am blessed to have worked alongside their Club Directors and their staff, the city officials, the local schools, parents and guardians, and the other community agencies. Together, we impacted over 2,100 K-12th grade members in our afterschool and summer programs annually.

Around the early part of May, we implemented my idea for an area milestone ceremony. For the last three years, we have recognized our young people who achieved the following academic targets:

• 5th graders moving on to middle school.

• 8th graders moving on to high school.

• 12th graders graduating from high school.

We announced each of our seniors' post-secondary plans which also served as a symbolic way for the underclassmen (K-11th graders) in the audience, to witness the end results of being an active member. It also indicated the conclusion of being a Boys & Girls Clubs member (the finale for seniors).

You could compare the program's culture to a shared mood and the climate to a shared lifestyle. Both cases require modeling to begin at the top. While in my position, I used a two-fold strategy: daily morning text messages to staff and monthly meetings with students in small groups divided by gender and grade. In these meetings, we discussed a variety of topics and continued to improve the culture and climate.

But believe me, this was not how it started. Let's go back to 2020 when I arrived at Palm Beach County. In the Glades, an area on the west side of the county known to be reclusive. If you are not familiar with the area, you would not know that it is a part of the county. And many people did not take in outsiders well.

I knew not to come in barking, but to observe. To learn. To fit in. Discover their trends. I started with the Advanced Insights Assessment and facilitated a Welcome 2 the Jungle® workshop. Do you recall how I invested in the personal, professional, and leadership development training I spoke of in chapter one? Back then, taking the sole responsibility to become the difference had just begun. But now, I shared the information confidently and helped transform the staff into a powerful team.

Through the assessment, once I distinguished my team members, I ascertained their strengths and weaknesses, in addition to learning their history and the community's background. When I discovered the staff averaged fifteen years of service at the facility, I got excited.

They had to know some things. Most had lived their entire life in the Glades area. One had been an assistant football coach before, served on the Deacon board at his local church, and had gone to school with all the pastors in the community.

As an outsider wanting in, wisdom called for me to leverage the relationships on my team. Get others to teach me the culture and how to detect the climate, which opened doors and allowed me to build relationships that benefited the organization, and ultimately the youth and teens we served.

Understand that big things didn't happen overnight. It took work. For three-and-a-half years, I communicated the vision, walked in the mission, and labored with my staff to implement the action steps.

In the beginning, *'I ain't go outside,'* as my young folks say. "Anthony Davis believes in building from the inside, first." It took me going back to the brand. "Let's work the forty-five students we have and, impact them." I instructed the team.

We treated those forty-five kids like they were the core of everything. And they started telling their friends about the elevator, the new studio where they could make their music, the music-math classes. We blended their culture with education while providing a safe, fun climate for all. Word of mouth spread that we were the place to be. Kids were excited and our membership grew—45 students grew to 95, and then within a few months, 240, exceeding our target daily attendance goal.

Vetted staff used their established connections to spread the word outside, selling our service, causing annual memberships to increase.

You know you've done something right when the principals call and ask what you're doing, encouraging you to keep doing it because their student's behavior and grades are improving from the kids' involvement with our program services.

How do students perceive, hear, feel, and act as they enter your daily afterschool or summer program? What affect do their actions have on the program's culture? As the leader, what can you do to ensure the standard of excellence is at the forefront of the organization or program's focus?

LESSON: As a leader, you can positively impact the culture and climate of your work location. This can be done by promoting a positive, inviting culture, setting high standards for student and staff behavior, and fostering a sense of community from the inside out.

When you create a panoptic culture, you make most young people and adults feel welcomed and valued. Go the extra steps to introduce communication tools to the team and educate them on how to ensure differing personalities feel heard (have a voice) in decision-making, celebrating diversity, and promote involvement in program activities.

CHALLENGE: Set high standards for youth behavior and create a respectful and safe environment. Communicate clear expectations, provide consistent consequences for misbehavior, and teach young people how to manage their emotions, and to resolve conflict peacefully.

Fostering a sense of community helps kids feel connected to your program, providing a safe haven. It also allows them to feel connected to each other.

"Good leadership is not necessarily about figuring out how to improve those around you; it's about creating a positive environment where those around you can improve themselves."
~ Carhsea Mitchell

Your leadership impacts the social-emotional needs of the young people you serve.

Whenever I visit a school, I look for evidence that the principal is focused on meeting the students' social-emotional needs. This can be as simple as greeting students with the correct pronunciation of their name as they arrive at your site location. Or, while delivering an uplifting and empowering message over the PA system every morning.

I have always chosen to work in urban schools and youth organizations with students of color from high-poverty environments, as I feel these schools can benefit the most from my specific skillset of innovating service ideas that yield win-win results for the agency and community. What a privilege to inspire people to work together while receiving personal professional fulfillment.

Too often though, the home experiences of students from these schools are unimaginable to educators and staff. This disconnect has profound implications for school leadership because these same children walk through your front doors daily, carrying their pain along with them. It's imperative we show them they are the future leaders of their families who can change things, change their environments, change themselves for the better.

Let's talk about the teen program dance fundraiser. We'd already hosted successful elementary dances in other communities and covered 100% of their membership fees to gain admission to all the after-school program services, so I thought to do the same for the older kids. It was that, or risk being held accountable for fulfilling the financial (membership fee) loss for the 220 teenagers.

But a dance for the teens came with many more obstacles. We'd have to address the gang problems in Belle Glade and Pahokee. How could we assure the kids safety? The event would take place during the Muck Bowl, the football game of the year. School ended early. Tailgating started at 2:30 p.m.

When I recommended the teen event a few months earlier to the board, they were very hesitant. I was unaware the young man pictured in the gym had been killed at the last dance, five years prior. Still, this leadership moment could impact the social-emotional needs of our students. A perfect opportunity to encourage a new mindset toward living their life in a way that set them up for a better future, while directing them away from the past.

I contacted the sheriff's department captain. He was one of the first people on the scene when the young man was killed. He knew his community. He'd know if I was being too ambitious. But if he could see the same vision, I believed we could overcome any obstacle.

The sheriff was like, "Anthony, you got to guarantee me nothing's going to happen."

An assurance rose in me, and I looked him square in his eyes. "I will have all seventy-five staff members working the event. We are going to check everybody. And ain't nothing gonna happen." Not because I had the power to do anything. But because I knew Who I was putting my trust in. I knew Who was able to protect His own. His blessed assurance was mine.

And he said, "All right, I'll take it to the city."

The mayor also hesitated over the idea of another teen dance. The death of that young man affected the core of this community. The loss hit deeply. They hadn't had a dance or gathering since. I wasn't aware my suggestion would peel layers from a wound still festering and in need of healing. Once the problem was exposed, my heart was set to be there throughout the toughest process. And even after the worst parts healed, I wanted to be there, applying a balm to each layer of the scar in the shape of quiet leadership and friendship until completely recovered.

I'd written the vision, planned tasks, and presented it to staff and every leader I would need to pull off the event of the year. That meant reaching out to the two schools and getting the leaders of every sport, club, squad, most popular, the best dressed, and any other identified leadership roles onboard.

Both schools' students said, "We think we can do this."

I challenged the principals to back their student body leaders. "I need you guys to promote it positively." And they did just that.

On the night of the Muck Bowl game, the town was buzzing with excitement, swelling by 25,000 extra fans. Think about it: Florida has over two hundred NFL players right now. Now, picture a scene where a bunch of these NFL pros, plus some retired ones, come together to watch one of the country's biggest high school football rivalries. It's not just a regular event—it's a big deal that everyone's talking about. And you bet the top college scouts from Division I (Power Five) schools are there, eager to spot the next football superstar in the making.

The dance was set to start at 7:30 p.m. By the third quarter, the home team was getting blown out and people were leaving. Teenagers looking for somewhere to go, found their way to the facility for the dance, paid the $7 entry fee, and checked in.

They had to have their school ID, and most used their phones to provide the verification. By 7:45 p.m. we had about fifty students. The D.J. had the music pumping and lights flickering. We had the 360-degree picture booth. Then, the D.J. went Facebook LIVE. And the kids already inside the dance went LIVE. All the stragglers from the blown-out game were drawn to the action.

Into the night we had over 300 teenagers in that gym. Even I got caught up in the dance contests. Whose knees can resist the Tootsie Roll? Adults and kids alike were having a blast. We had a team of law enforcement in place, providing continued surveillance to ensure safety, but not so invasive to take from the festivities.

Again, 300 teenagers from across town, to rivals, to members of gangs were in the gym. We would've loved to accommodate more, but the crowd was just right for us, especially nearing midnight, close to the end of the dance. Unfortunately, we had to turn some people away.

No problem. We had done what we set out to do.

The mayor arrived to witness the gathering of both schools getting along after five years. He shed tears of joy over the moment of resolution. The same night, he called me and said, "I'm so proud of you guys for doing that." That was Friday.

Monday hit. I went in by 10 a.m. The kids were spreading the word, branding us as the cool place to be. A *safe* place to be. Membership increased. Even the principals from both schools called. "Man, we need to do another. It's all the kids are talking about."

So, let me ask you: Are the social-emotional needs of your students being met in your program? Are they a priority under your leadership? Are structures in place to ensure students' emotional safety and security? What programs are set up for your students to help meet the students' needs?

Peer counseling and restorative practices, two programs I have liked over the years, enable students to be deeply engaged with one another in a variety of different situations are.

LESSON: Leaders of all ages, at every level, significantly impact the social-emotional needs of the students in your program. Students look up to leaders as role models and will emulate their behavior. If a leader maintains a sense of calm and control during times of stress, your students will likely do the same. On the other hand, if that leader tends to lash out or become frazzled quickly, don't be surprised when your students adopt similar behaviors. It is essential to be aware of your student's social-emotional needs. Unmet necessities can lead to behavioral problems and a decline in academic performance and social-emotional learning opportunities.

CHALLENGE: Meet the social-emotional needs of your students. Here are a few ways to get started:

• Ensure a safe and supportive environment.

• Identify leaders and involve them when planning student activities.

• Help your students develop a positive sense of self-esteem and confidence.

• Encourage your students to express their feelings.

• Help them develop positive relationships with their peers.

• Teach students how to deal with stress and anxiety effectively.

• Help your students develop a positive outlook on life.

• Set clear expectations and rules.

• Model to students how to be respectful and kind to one another.

• Help the student identify and express their emotions in a healthy way.

> *"Encouragement is the greatest form of motivation. Never underestimate the power of your words."*
> *~ Kyle Hunt*

LIVE BY INTEGRITY: MISSION, VALUES & PURPOSE

4

LEADERSHIP: IT'S A MINDSET WORTH MORE THAN MONEY

*T*he mission and the tasks: What role do they play in the mindset of leadership?

You cannot mistake your personal mission for your role responsibilities. The latter requires endless paperwork, interminable meetings, planning, administrative duties, and so many other little jobs. Identifying the most critical tasks is important to any plans you have in place to improve the quality of your youth program. However, when your work meshes well with your own belief system, far less burnout and dissatisfaction occur.

When faced with so many responsibilities, stress is unavoidable, but realizing the value of your personal mission will sustain you. Discover the specific tasks that speak your name and answer why you choose to work with kids, and you will no longer see your position as a job but a calling. This mindset shift is a game changer. It has the power to motivate you to inspire student excellence even when you believe you have little to offer, feel overwhelmed, or sometimes become discouraged with the process.

In 2010, I planned a self-esteem workshop specifically for teenage girls. This was a first. With no prior example to go by, I lacked my usual confidence, but my personal mission to protect, empower, and teach kids they are somebody no matter their situation, pushed me to look past my inadequacies and complete the task. I never wanted to turn my back on any child in need. While I would never know what it meant to be a young, teenaged girl, to empathize effectively, I had to revisit common uncertainties all youth face.

As a teenager, I had to learn I have a choice to succeed. Suffering low self-esteem being a seventh grader, reading at a third-grade level, I covered my inadequacies with charm and acting the class clown. Considering these were universal struggles, the mission helped me to embrace the tasks it would take to make the workshop a success.

It's opportunities like these, that will reveal the benefits of tapping into your personal mission to drive you forward.

Having been that kid who lived in a homeless shelter, dependent on adults to make decisions—hopefully in my best interest, I wanted the girls to play an active role in the decision-making process. Instead of organizing events the adults thought might work, I started conversations with the girls to determine what they wanted. Then, I questioned their parents for another point-of-view. Together, we planned an event with 100% female role models. In an effort to remove any limiting beliefs, we contacted women from the local area who worked in career fields dominated by men to be our guest speakers. A CEO, CFO, pharmacist, DJ, and a player in the WNBA represented their fields at the workshop, breaking the stereotypes. The young ladies benefited greatly. In many of our facilities, the program is still taking place.

LESSON: Don't allow doubts to keep you from taking on tasks outside your immediate wheelhouse. Confident leaders are not born …but built from taking on new tasks and completing them. The more you succeed the more confident you become in doing it again, and again. And when you see how your efforts helped others, your confidence is reinforced.

To overcome the initial fear, realize and tap into your personal mission to relate to your kids' needs. This extra effort will benefit you as much as your students, especially, youth deemed as "at-risk."

What is your personal mission? Which are your most passionate role responsibilities, and why? What specific role will you play in your students' transformation to be the difference and lead with confidence?

CHALLENGE: Shift your mindset and turn the job into your calling. Identify the personal mission driving you to lead youth and allow it to produce your best work.

> *"It's good to have high expectations of others. It's more imperative that we have high expectations of ourselves."*
> *~ Imelda Rodriguez*

What fuels your passion for leadership?

All jobs come with pros and cons.

A recent search of Indeed.com's employee reviews of the Boys & Girls Clubs of America Unit Director's position gave me a new mission as a fellow youth leader. The comments ran the gamut from singing praises to condemnation. I was moved to encourage my fellow leaders to take charge and learn what fuels their desire to show up each day and lead effectively. Thereby, turning more of those negative comments to positives.

Start by finding your motivators. The Advanced Insights Profile is a tool that addresses seven dimensions of value, but in the following example, we will use my top two—political and altruist.

My political scores revealed I am very passionate about opportunities to lead and take control of a variety of initiatives. Then, there is my empathy for others' needs which also scored very high. Therefore, it's easy to conclude a position that limits my ability to render aid would be torturous. Based on this information, not receiving the call from the NFL was the best thing to ever happen.

Not making this prestigious appointment but working with kids who shared my upbringing and look like me, led me to the greatest work of my career. As I mentioned earlier, when your job is aligned with your natural beliefs, there is less resistance to perform tasks, which reduces the stress that robs from your energy banks.

With this knowledge in mind, I have purposed in my heart to show up every day and lead because I am blessed to make a decent living for my family doing what I love. My role responsibilities perfectly align to motivate me to be my best. This doesn't stop some days from being harder than others, but in leadership, we must work to create rewarding moments to renew our passion to serve the kids.

If you recall my high school days as an ambassador, reading at the elementary, my motivators explain why helping a child in need ignites an endless source of passion. One such instance was the summer of 2013. We had the opportunity to bring fifty homeless, at-risk youth into the organization's summer program. I experienced my childhood all over again. Although it awakened my soul wound, I didn't have to be the helpless young man who watched his father drive away, leaving his sons to play football in a parking lot of a homeless shelter we never should have had to call home. But you will learn more about this in the next chapter.

The closest facility to us at the shelter would have been about seven miles away, so it wasn't an option for me and my brother. But giving these kids the summer program opportunity was a step toward an internal healing I didn't know I needed.

It would take fifty-thousand dollars to cover ten weeks of summer memberships, field trips, transportation, meals, and all the bells and whistles. I was passionate about finding a donor.

When speaking with our executive board of directors, some might think the passion to help at-risk children is naturally shared by everyone. But I believe their excitement had more to do with a clear vision articulated well. The board members connected with their friends and shared the vision, inspiring some to write checks.

Some benefactors did not donate, but you should expect to get nos. Don't discredit them and burn a bridge, but understand they are unable to support you in this season. Keep articulating the vision. "For every ten you may get two" is an old saying among those in the sales profession. The ones who are supposed to support you, do. Thinking a "no" is simply your next opportunity helps you keep a genuine smile on your face and fosters the courage to engage your next possible donor. Think, "rejection is direction." Why? Because you cannot afford to let negative thoughts reduce the potency of your passion.

LESSON: We are programmed with natural motivators that fuel our passion to perform well, because all jobs come with pros and cons. Times will call for you to create rewarding moments. Prepare to adopt a "Where there is a will, there is a way" mindset.

We then partnered with the Education Foundation. Much like the school principal had advised earlier in this book, I learned what this organization could use from the services the Boys & Girls Clubs offered. What was their role in the lives of these kids? How could we help the Education Foundation fulfill their goals? Unsurprisingly, most of the organization's needs centered around education and once again, we infused their goals into our summer program and received the funding.

As a result, kids who usually went without dinner during the summer months received enough food to eat and share with family. For the first time in our history, a 55-passenger charter bus transported the kids every day. Moments like these remind me why I need to show up ready to work. I do not live for myself, but for others.

The young people's resilience also motivates me to lead each day. I am always amazed at their ability to face obstacles and persevere in difficult situations. Kids can overcome challenges and still achieve great things when they believe in themselves. The power of belief is something I work to instill in every young person I'm blessed to influence. It is one of the most rewarding aspects of my personal mission.

It is truly satisfying to observe a youth who doubted their ability to succeed at school or in a sport become motivated and confident. To have proof of the transformative power education and after-school programs have on youth gives my work purpose. This is why I am passionate about helping them achieve their educational, career, and life goals. I believe every child, no matter their age, can succeed with the proper support and resources.

When did you first realize you wanted the role of a leader? You were driven by something, right? What compels you now? How will that motivator help the youth you serve to succeed?

Passion is like a vehicle that needs fuel to keep it going. Do you worry your students will not apply themselves in life if they don't have the guidance you can offer? Do you want to create an after-school program that is peaceful, calm, and focuses on students who have chaotic homes or emotional needs? Examine the primary catalyst that will drive you to pursue your leadership career.

CHALLENGE: All kids need a champion to encourage them to win. Please, go out and show them the way. That champion is you, and it is important that you refuel to be able to serve. Sometimes that means seeking a moment that renews your passion to help them. Dig deep if you must, even if that moment takes facing your childhood struggles to ignite your passion and motivate you into action.

Do not let up. Period.

"It doesn't matter what kind of after-school program you have. The success of your program is a result of the adults leading it. Adults are always the variable."
~ Terrance Johnson

Does your leadership align with your personal mission?

Have you met that youth leader who talks about their accomplishments for hours, but their actions do not align with their message? What we believe must be expressed in our actions as a leader if we are to crack the tough cases and really make a difference in our communities, schools, and the lives of the kids.

I believe there are three Cs every youth leader must master to experience true alignment with their mission:

• **Competence** – Combining your skills, knowledge, behavior, or attitude to perform your role responsibilities well.

• **Commitment** – Dedication to the community, beyond your program's duties.

• **Character** – Modeling authenticity to influence change in a child's life.

If ever there was a student's life I wanted to save, it was Chantoni Grant's. Not like God, who has power over death, but to spare this young man the unnecessary hardships I suffered. We were first introduced at the end of his freshman year of high school. He was not performing well academically. His coach knew about our after-school program and believed Chantoni would benefit from the services. Also, we had programs to keep the young man too busy to get into trouble.

Back when I was a Program Director, I made it a point to review report cards. Without fail, the boys from African

American and Latino families performed significantly lower than their counterparts on a consistent basis.

Why?

Searching for the answer sent me on a journey that shifted my initial leadership mission to simply empower these boys. Empowerment was not enough without tangible results, though. Kids who were exposed to the same teachers, curriculum, and programs should have similar academic performance scores.

But how to get them?

The only factor that differed among them was where the kids spent their time after they left us. I now understand how God used my connection with Chantoni and his need for a positive outlet to develop me further as a leader, equipping me with competence, commitment, and character. I would have to lead from a vulnerable place, be who I wanted to see him become, and search my own past to guide me to the answers.

Chantoni was a lot like the younger me—made everyone laugh. Where I am a middle child, he is the oldest of his siblings. His mother, like mine, was a single parent with limited means. He would physically tackle anything that moved. But when answering a question on a piece of paper, he acted as if he feared it would bite him. Sitting still and having to test … he'd remain in a state of shock. He was very talented in many areas, as much as any of his counterparts, but going from house to house, not having a place to belong … I knew that strain. A strain that affected my grades, so I understood his struggles.

I knew what it was like to live with the pressure of taking on the role of a man and the father-figure, providing and protecting my entire family years before I was mentally, physically, or emotionally ready. And I assumed Chantoni dealt with much of the same.

When kids were supposed to be thinking of attending homecoming, prom, and hanging with friends, youth like Chantoni were lost in thought, worrying during class about how the light bill would get paid or if there would be anything to eat when they got home. This kind of stress is a breeding ground for test anxiety.

This is why your specific leadership mission is so important. It is why I encourage you to hang in there and be the difference. We all come with unique experiences God has used to shape and build our characters to help someone else.

Trying to reach Chantoni left me with the first order of business—to build trust. Here you'll see competence in effect while operating in full transparency. That meant delivering on all that I said I'd do, modeling the very character Chantoni would need to adopt to turn things around in his own life.

Then, I had to show up. He had to get used to seeing me, on campus, in the community, at the facility. Only when he believed I was more than a director on payroll, invested in him, would I be able to influence him. And supporting his mom with the tangibles worked to accelerate the process.

A mom's needs are simple. *Take care of my baby.* Chantoni was thirteen years older than his siblings and he was literally eating her out of house and home. What single parent's budget wouldn't benefit from someone feeding their teenaged athlete, who is burning calories and always hungry? And everyone in the education arena knows how a balanced meal can make a difference when it comes to low academic performance and behavior issues. With the help of my wife, Ericka, we made sure he ate well and had snacks every growing boy needs. Then, when work did not permit his mother to be involved, we showed up, supplementing the lack without replacing her. I coached him as Lawrence Fishburne did for Keke Palmer in the movie *Akeelah and the Bee*.

I still marvel at how much his life mirrored my own. Chantoni never knew his dad. I knew I was not there to replace the idea of his father, but to provide the male guidance a young man seeks at the crucial stages of life. Times when he would make decisions that affect his future. I know this because of the mentors, teachers, and educators who did the same for me at that tender age. Roderick M. Smith Sr., Ricky Smith, Marcus Singleton, Brian Coe, Sterling Frederick, Verryl Floyd… A few names among many I could mention.

When Chantoni made an F, I met with his teachers, coach, and principal. Considering his tendencies, and by adopting an approach a positive role model used with me at that age, I strategically roped off every exit and direction he thought he might take. I spoke with directors, guidance counselors, and his instructors. We created a plan—he would be redirected to me for any, and all disciplinary infractions. If he was late for class, or skipped football practice, I was the first to know. He knew we shared the same story, so when discipline came from me, he had no excuses, no outs. Even when it took taking him back to school and working with a tutor, we teamed up to make sure he got there.

I once kicked the front door in at Chantoni's house. Not literally, but I created a ruckus, enough noise to make sure somebody came to the door. It may seem extreme in this day and time, but I refused to watch him fail no matter how society accepted it based on his zip code and economic level. Behavior issues and lower-performing students generally lead people to expect less of them. I will be the first to tell you, sometimes, blinded by my personal mission, I have not done everything perfect. I've missed the mark plenty of times, but in this case, I answered yes to the call on my life. Chantoni went from a 1.8 GPA to a 3.0 and higher by his senior year. He transformed into a young man of character before my eyes.

He honored me when I walked him on the field his Senior night. I was there on decision day. When he struggled with if he should go off to school when he did not receive a scholarship offer near home, he sought me for guidance because I had earned his trust all those years ago.

He accepted the scholarship offer that took him to North Carolina Wesleyan University, NCWU, in Rocky Mount, North Carolina. Every Christmas, Thanksgiving, and other holiday breaks, he called me to pick him up from the train station and we hung out. I would go to where his mom and siblings were. I had promised to show up. My commitment did not conveniently end when he went away for college.

Chantoni debated if he should come home after graduating with his bachelor's or get his master's degree. You know I told him to go for it. He had scholarships that covered 75% of his tuition, but he had to come up with the remaining 25%. His advisor told him about seeking an internship with the Boys & Girls Clubs organization there to cover the remaining expenses.

The CEO over that facility, was none other than my mentor, Ron Green. Today, Chantoni has his master's degree from Full Sail University in Orlando, Florida just forty minutes north from where our father-son relationship started. Like me, he waited for the NFL to call after college, but when they did not, he again contacted me for advice. I told him to go for it and Chantoni accepted the pivot. Today, he is the director of the Bishop Esports at NCWU. His company creates the majority of video games for console systems like PlayStation.

God had it set up for him the entire time. We still talk to this day, but I'll never forget the day he told me, "Thank you. You went over and beyond your job. I know it was a God thing."

LESSON: Here are a few key characteristics of aligning your leadership with your mission. Be someone who can take on challenging tasks and see them through to the end. Your role consists of building strong, trusting relationships with competence, commitment, and character. You can be confident that you're making the best choices for your staff and the kids you serve.

CHALLENGE: Give 120% daily. Remember, talk is cheap.

You get nothing done by giving excuses, but you are viewed in high regard when you execute.

"Program leaders are more motivated when their administration supports them, values them, and encourages them. Guess when youth and teens are more motivated?"
~ Tiffany Frederick

Leadership ensuring the program's safety mission.

In recent years, school and after-school program leaders have been under increasing pressure to ensure the safety of their students. This is due to the escalating number of mass shootings widely reported. Some were nearby. Some far. With the power of social media, we can know when terror strikes within seconds.

In 2018, just sixty-eight miles south of where I worked with youth in Indiantown, FL, the Stoneman Douglas High School shooting occurred in Parkland, Florida. My heart shattered, especially after being a guest speaker at an MLK event, connecting with over 300 high school students from Broward County Public Schools just two weeks prior. I vividly recall the great conversations I had with several students from Stoneman Douglas High. But I would have had the same response had I not visited the site location.

I am not here to cast blame or point fingers, but I have a question. What must we do to ensure the safety of our children? Where is the security mechanism in front of their homes, schools, after-school programs, churches, parks, stores, etc.?

Although we cannot guarantee that every student will be safe from a catastrophic event, it is part of the mission of any leader to do all within their power to ensure students are protected, to the best of their ability, in a severe emergency. School principals and after-school programs should create, distribute, and discuss a plan for crisis management that addresses as many contingencies as possible on a regular basis.

As the leader, you need to ask yourself the following questions: Is everyone on staff aware of their role in an emergency? Are all staff members conversant with the details of the plan? What about the youth? Do they know what their roles are in different situations? Are the emergency plans executed efficiently? Does your program location hold emergency drills? How does your program or organization communicate with local hospitals and law enforcement?

Although I'm certain many youth members and staff were annoyed by the numerous lockdown drills during my time as an Executive Club Director, executing our emergency plan as close to perfection as possible was the goal.

LESSON: True safety takes repetition until the proper responses become second nature. Drills are there for this purpose, after all. In this case, the challenge must come first. We cannot afford for any child in our care to learn this lesson the hard way.

The location manager must ensure their facility or program area is a safe and secure environment for youth and staff. Ways to measure whether an organization meets this goal, include studying data on violent incidents, tracking changes in program climate surveys, and observing modulation in student and staff behavior.

Collecting data and evidence from various sources is essential to determine whether you are achieving your program safety leadership mission. This will give you a well-rounded picture of how your operation is doing in terms of safety and security.

CHALLENGE: Have a preventive action plan and practice the drill often. It is essential.

"Relationships are not generated out of thin air; they are cultivated through genuine conversations ... and are made stronger through vulnerability."
~ Ken Funderburk

5

POWER OF PURPOSE

*W*hat is your purpose as a leader?

Your leadership purpose is not to be confused with your mission, although it is just as important.

Mission is "why" your organization exists and why you are the perfect person to do things the way you do them to get their goals accomplished. Knowing your why keeps you going over the long haul. Even in the roughest of times.

Purpose is "how" you lead to get results. Some of you create team strategies to get the job done. Others, leads by example. Then there are those who have the Deion Sanders mindset, the "Prime Effect," and speak inspiration that fuels people into action.

Protecting and empowering the children in my after-school program made me show up after a recent lockdown for active gunshots at four of the twenty facilities I oversee. Yes, I could have settled for the phone call with local law enforcement and staff who have been trained to handle situations like these.

However, I needed the staff, kids, and parents to see that I trust the systems we have in place to keep them safe. I wanted all to know I am there for them and would not ask anyone to return to an environment I had not investigated personally.

If you're like me, your personal experiences helped shape your leadership. I recall one such shaping experience vividly. It was the worst days of my life.

I grew up in a gated community with green grass, trimmed hedges, and smooth even landscaping. It had a little playground and everything. The air smelled good and sweet.

Only one thing was wrong with it. It was not a home. It was the homeless shelter.

Me and my little brother, nine years younger, would set up these little orange cones to practice my football drills in an area near the parking lot. The cones were about six inches higher than the ground. I did a simple workout on the pavement because the shelter did not have much grass. And we used stones for markers. My brother would throw me the ball.

While running drills, I imagined myself away from there. Tried to see myself in a stadium. Envisioned myself getting better as I completed the workout. I had stopped to catch my breath and took a swig from my water bottle when I heard a beeping sound of a truck.

Beep-beep, again.

A cream Isuzu with a flatbed drew closer.

It was my father.

He blew the horn and threw his deuces up, like I was his homeboy. And he kept going, knowing we were living at a homeless shelter.

I stood there and watched until his taillights faded out of sight.

I told myself, "I'll be da*ned if I ever let that happen, again. Ever!" Today, as an adult, I use how I felt in that moment as a kid to shape my "why" and guide me in the way I show up for the kids who share similar stories. Not bitter, but better by the grace of God, for having overcome the struggle and experienced healing.

But for the "how," I must take you back to my school days and credit Ms. Nadilia Charles in addition to my lessons from Andrew.

Ms. Charles was about four feet nine inches tall. She put you in the mind of the Sister Souljah activist type, a spiritual warrior for that which is right. When she saw potential in you, she did not allow any of your foolish or disruptive behavior to deter her mission of bringing the best out of you.

Fall of 1998, I was in Ms. Charles' seventh grade. She was a first-year teacher, and graduate, straight out of Florida A&M University, FAMU. Ms. Charles introduced herself with confidence, as if she wasn't fresh meat. She tried to set the tone like she was somebody, but her delivery conflicted with her small stature.

Some classmates and I made a pact to take her through the test and show her who was really running things. What I did not count on was Ms. Charles caring enough to study our student profiles to learn more about us individually—information she would use to stay one step ahead of our divisive plans.

I cracked jokes on Ms. Charles about her height. Her voice. Anything to disrupt the class, to get everybody to laugh at her. I would back off before things went too far, though. My way of being somewhat respectful, even if I was being *disrespectful*. I never cursed her although some of my friends did. That was too extreme in my book.

But the day came when I became disruptive with my jokes. Sister-girl pushed back and called me out in class. I stood up to her and was like, "What you say?" as I went up to her and faced off.

Ms. Charles was from the Miami, Florida, 305 area code, all the way live, exhibiting a stance I was familiar with. She had no plans of backing down. She demanded respect. Due to her height, she put her head right in the middle of my chest and said, "Boy, you're going to sit down and read this book."

Every time I cracked jokes, Ms. Charles called for the class to pull out a book. She would assign two pages. Everyone took a turn, reading a paragraph or two. While they read, I pre-read my pages so the rest of the class would not realize how hard I struggled to pronounce the words, comprehending even less.

The day came when she called on me to read right away, rather than being one of the last readers. With no time to prepare, you can imagine how horrible I read. She repeated this a few times until I stayed after class and asked, "Why are you doing this to me?"

"Why are you doing this to *me*?" She kept answering my question with a question of her own.

"Why do you keep making fun of me?"

"Why do you keep getting your friends to laugh at me and disrupt my classroom?" She had a comeback for everything I threw at her.

"Because it's funny," I said.

"And that's why I keep calling you to read and let you struggle in front of your so-called friends. If you noticed, everybody is laughing at you, not me."

For the first time, I sat back, and I was like, *oh ... the joke is on me.*

"I have a college degree, and I want to ensure you receive what you need. Stop letting people boost your head up, knowing good and well you don't know the essentials." She paused, as if allowing me time to accept the truce she offered. "You're trying to get where I am, but don't know the way. Let me show you."

I stopped fighting her, and she worked with me, building my confidence first. She knew I loved sports and would bring me stories with pictures. My favorite athlete was Deion Sanders. I will never forget the Sports Illustrated magazine with him on the front cover. (see toolbox for link.) We moved from reading magazines to little books, maybe fifteen pages. From fifteen, to thirty, to 100 pages and so on and so forth. That was her method to get me excited about what I was reading.

However, I still struggled. Fast forward, I went to high school.

I became popular in 2000, my freshman year at Santaluces Community High School where I took my first state exam. I was a freshman playing football on Varsity but was still not reading at grade level. I had a big head, but it was full of nothing. No real substance. Really good at math—I passed that portion. Calculating how to get past defenders was a breeze on the field, but I still could not manage to tackle the reading portion of the exam in the classroom. Comprehension was still an issue. Why? I would later realize; I was taking the wrong angle.

The school districts restructured the zones, forcing me to transfer to Boynton Beach Community High, the new school. In the classroom, instead of working to grow from what Ms. Charles had taught me in the seventh grade, I charmed my teachers into letting me take oral exams on anything that required reading comprehension to pass. It is not surprising I failed the state exam three times, always the reading portion.

Fall of 2003, my senior year, it was the first day of school. I was leaning on the locker with my girl when I thought I heard a familiar voice call me. Ms. Charles? But I had transferred to the new school, so it couldn't be her.

"Ur, A. D." She knew how to draw out the "ur" to interrupt the conversation before pronouncing each initial of my name. "You ain't passed the FCAT." The Florida Comprehensive Assessment Test, state exam. I was too busy wondering why she was at my school and how she knew my business to respond. "You want to graduate high school?" She asked, obviously not caring the kids around me had stopped to gawk at me.

It was as if I was a seventh grader all over again. I finally answered. "Yes, of course."

"You better have your behind in my classroom every Friday at 4 o'clock." I later learned she had transferred and would be one of my teachers. Ms. Charles could care less when I told her that the group tutoring sessions conflicted with my football games on Fridays. Ms. Charles checked me quickly about my academic reality when I was trying to get her to understand the importance of my athletic world. Little did I know, I would not be the only one. Another teammate attended the same sessions. But you have to remember Ms. Charles was from the 3-0-5 area code. She did not care that we had a football game, she was calling her own plays—a by-any-means-necessary kind of teacher for all of her students.

Ms. Charles had been following my progress and took it upon herself to move to the high school and personally see to my preparation for the state exam.

Every Friday, when the last school bell rang at 2:15 p.m., I went and got my pregame meal. Then, I headed to the locker room, grabbed my uniform, and off to her room, leaving my teammates getting crunk to Lil Jon & The East Side Boyz, Trick Daddy and T.I., having fun.

Home games, I got on the field right at kickoff. Away games, she would ensure my teammates and I had adequate transportation to the game, but we usually arrived closer to the second quarter. And not one game did she feel sorry. Why? Her major concern was to make sure I passed Florida's state exam and received my high school diploma. Period.

During our study sessions, Ms. Charles provided a little booklet, teaching me the strategies on how to take a test and comprehend the why. We went deep. Talk about a tutor. She probably could charge thousands today for all the details she covered. She helped me identify my true strengths and areas of growth. But like any kid who is down on themselves and scared of failure, when things got tough, I gave up on the process and tested her one more time. I intentionally missed a Friday.

Monday morning, she showed up to my locker. She pulled me to the side and challenged me in a way only Ms. Charles would do it. She whispered a hard truth that resonated deeply. Her words, a gentle breeze of wisdom, but strong enough to stir me to my core. At that moment, the weight of an unspoken destiny descended upon me as though an impending storm brewed. She became my lighthouse, attempting to guide me through treacherous waters. Warning me, continuing the same path could lead me astray and shatter my dreams.

She used my fears to get my attention, causing me to rethink what was really important to me. Ms. Charles had not said anything I had not thought myself. She simply spoke my fears aloud. She was right. But the way she confronted me, she reminded me I had a choice set before me, and *I* was choosing to fail. After that, I never missed a Friday.

The test was in late November. In all my years of taking the state exams, I finally felt confident. I completed it. The results came back four months later. Ms. Charles was the first to ask had I gotten my scores. She was there crying in the background when I was told I passed all portions of the FCAT.

I later learned Ms. Charles had promised my grandmother, before she died, that I would graduate high school. She had arranged for all administration to contact her if I was late to class, not turning in my work, etc. before calling my house. Sound familiar? Does it remind you of the Chantoni story?

Never doubt your purpose as a leader, but let it fuel you to be the difference in a student's life. Ms. Charles was my guardian angel. Every opportunity I get to take the stage, I tell this story because of the tremendous impact she had on my life. Then, I thought she simply liked me, but now I know it was a strategy. A strategy I still duplicate with the kids in my programs.

Again, I ask you, what is your purpose as a leader? Ultimately, it comes down to your why, your values, and what you want to achieve in your role to determine the steps you will take to make things happen. For you, your students, and your community.

Are you looking to build a successful team or organization? How? Or are you looking to make a difference in your community or the world at large? Why? Are you looking to inspire others and create positive change?

LESSON: It is not enough to know "why" you do what you do, but we must gain clarity on "how" we will go about achieving our goals. As a leader, you have the unique opportunity to change things, save a life, and make a lasting impact on the world. Discovering what works best for you will take time and experience, so give yourself room to try things and fail so you can monitor and record the actions and activities that have the most impact for you, your team, and community.

Your purpose as a leader can be anything you want it to be. It all depends on what you're passionate about and the end-result you look to achieve. Once you have a clear purpose in mind, you can work toward it and make a difference in the world. Here are some ideas to help you decide how you will lead:

• **Setting Positive Examples**: Lead by example, demonstrating the values and behaviors you wish to instill in the people you work with. This includes modeling a positive attitude and honing your communication skills.

• **Building Relationships**: Prioritize building strong, positive relationships with the people you serve. Show genuine interest, actively listen to their concerns, and create a safe and supportive environment for transparent communication.

• **Empowering Others**: Believe in the potential of the people you work with and empower them to take on leadership roles and responsibilities. Encourage decision-making and problem-solving, fostering a sense of ownership.

• **Goal Setting**: Assist in setting realistic and achievable goals. Help create action plans to reach these goals, providing guidance and support along the way.

• **Skill Development**: Identify and nurture the talents and skills of the students and staff you work with. Provide opportunities for learning and growth, both in traditional educational areas and in essential life skills such as communication, teamwork, and resilience.

• **Cultural Competence**: Understand and respect the diverse backgrounds and experiences of those you serve. It is important you create an inclusive environment where staff, students, and parents feel welcomed, valued, and understood.

• **Advocacy**: Serve as advocates for the needs and interests of those who work with you. Connect them with resources and opportunities that have the potential to enrich their lives and provide support during challenging times.

• **Flexibility**: Good leaders recognize that each person is unique and may require different approaches. They are flexible in their methods, tailoring their strategies to meet the specific needs of the kids they work with.

• **Collaboration**: Collaborate with other organizations, agencies, and community members to create your support network. Build partnerships that offer a wide range of opportunities and resources for your organization.

• **Continuous Learning**: Be committed to your own growth and development. Stay informed about best practices in leadership, youth development, attend training and workshops, and seek feedback from peers and students to continually improve your leadership skills.

CHALLENGE: Play a pivotal role in nurturing the potential of the people you serve. Help them build self-confidence and prepare them for successful futures. By combining your leadership purpose with a genuine passion for empowering others, you can make a lasting impact on their lives.

Words cannot explain the fulfillment that comes from serving others. With Chantoni, my mission was to empower a young man of color, who also lived in a difficult situation, with support, tools, and the knowledge that he was somebody who deserved to succeed, like the next man. Why was this my mission? Why pursue this goal regardless of the obstacles?

Because the *data* showed a slight chance of advancement in situations like ours. But I am living proof that it *is* possible. I needed there to be evidence for the next director to keep working hard, because the kids were worth fighting for. My why would not allow me to accept no as the final answer for that young man. Naturally, my how wouldn't allow me to simply state what needed to be done while I felt called to jump out front to lead by example. If my actions could give life, direction, or motivate one kid to establish a pattern for success in the future, my past struggles were not in vain.

What is driving you to lead? What do you truly desire your leadership to accomplish? What is your top leadership priority? How will you lead?

"Good leaders trust their people. Period. If they don't … they will end up micromanaging, and that sabotages morale."
~ Jaylynn Christie

What evidence supports your leadership purpose?

While we all want to believe we are effective leaders, do our results show our efforts are making a real difference in the lives of youth? In other words, prove it! Prove you have done everything you can. Anyone can state all they have done to reach their goals and conclude it is impossible. But what story does your daily walk tell? What are others saying about you?

Even now, you will see me in the streets. I don't know how to turn my back on children and drive away without letting them know someone not only sees them but cares enough to do something about their situation. If we mean to empower and save these kids' lives, it will require us to go outside the walls of the facilities and sometimes beyond the responsibilities listed in our job descriptions.

Like my mentors, I have worked so community members can say they saw me at our neighborhood churches. At the school, recitals, and football games. My job responsibilities only require me to be at the facility when the kids get there at 2:30 p.m. and after school until 8:00 p.m. However, I go outside the walls because I actually care. Why do anything halfway?

But I would be remiss if I did not caution you to develop a balance between your professional and personal life. When you have a family, what you are willing to do for the youth you serve, must be done in your home first. The best, who lead by example, do it in every part of their lives or risk destroying the very example they are trying to set for others. Ask any pastor who has fallen before his congregation. Years of great service can be destroyed with one act that resulted from not taking care of their personal lives.

In this, I have failed.

I spent so much time looking back at my past and where I did not want to be, I wound up doing the very things to my own kids I had spent my life running from.

Confession time. In 2014, my marriage was tested. My travel schedule had picked up heavily. I took on more kids and their situations. My wife contacted me, and said, "I did not sign up to raise our child by myself."

What a blow. I was providing a roof over my family's head. We were eating right. How could she insinuate I was an absentee father? She knew my past.

Now, I didn't disrespect her, but it was more like, *yo, this is where we have to separate, in a sense.* To make her feel bad, I was quick to remind her how she'd grown up in the penthouse. I complained she did not know what she was talking about. I had a just-let-me-be-me attitude. Let me lead this ship even if I was only doing the basics.

You see, I married up. Her father had set the bar of expectation high, and I felt she was saying I was not making the mark. Today, I know she was right. Coming from generations of broken families, I did not have a true example. As long as I provided more than what I had grown up with, I believed I was doing good. But Ericka was pushing me to be better, when I was resistant to that push.

It didn't sink in until a close friend pulled me to the side and said, "Bro. you're turning into your dad. Everything you said he did, you're doing it."

I was angry enough to want to hit him. But this was the same guy who had witnessed everything and had to bear my complaints over the years.

Ericka had said the same thing in so many words, but it was easy to tune her out. She had never been in my shoes. She'd been spoiled, came from the ideal home with a mom and dad. But when my friend who shared my upbringing called me out, the excuses in my head no longer worked.

When two or three are saying the same thing, it's hard not to listen.

LESSON: Look to the evidence to prove you are in alignment with your leadership purpose. It doesn't take someone coming from the same socioeconomic background to recognize when there are character issues that need to be addressed. Character is universal for all humans. Any two or three people saying the same thing is cause for you to stop and reevaluate what you are thinking.

If you recall, taking time out to reflect helps me see things clear of emotions, so I can focus on the facts. I wrote some stuff down and searched inwardly.

Even if my line of work was legal, I found I had a lot in common with my father. We shared similar behaviors and thought patterns, always working at the cost of our family. Even affection had been supplemented in my home with "You've got lights, you've got water, the mortgage is paid…" My family had Dasani water.

Knowing I needed someone who would call me out on my excuses, I hired a coach who was not connected to me personally. He was married and held couples' classes. Coach K, of

Grindation LLC, helped me find balance and a rhythm with life, becoming my example of a successful businessman who understood how his personal life played a major role in that success. I needed to become a better man at home.

CHALLENGE: Your personal life is directly connected to your professional success. Learn from my regrets and take five minutes to list all the activities you've done to reach your goals for the year, personally and professionally. After reflecting on the evidence, is there proof you are leading well? And if not, what are you willing to do to change things? It is good to have people in your immediate circle who are not afraid to call you out and disagree with you.

"I think senior management (C-Suite) should connect with kids … but they should also connect with their front-line staff. Yes, staff need their support and encouragement too."
- Arielle Curate

Your leadership purpose affects the performance of the staff and young people you serve.

When I visit after-school programs, like Boys & Girls Clubs, YMCA, Urban League, etc., I look for signs of purpose and action in adult leaders, students, staff, and faculty inter-actions.

I once visited an organization in Georgia. The Assistant Site Director showed me around the building. He seemed nervous when we entered the classrooms where programs were being conducted.

It became apparent he was used to entering the building to discipline students, instead of ensuring the kids were being served. I felt sorry for him. When a leader's responsibilities are limited to disciplining students, in my experience, they are usually poor youth development professionals.

In a sidebar conversation, I asked what motivated him to become a youth leader. I believed him when he told me he wanted to help children find hope, but he did not feel he was living his purpose. The organization's culture had made him a full-time disciplinarian, and he had lost his way.

I asked him if he and the Site Director, his immediate supervisor, had discussed other requirements of his role. As I suspected, he said, "no." He explained how he felt trapped and could not do much to change his current role. Not only was this a disservice to him, but also for the children and program assistants he supervised. With his focus solely on discipline, how was he to accurately assess staff and contribute to everyone's professional development?

LESSON: Communication with supervision should include role responsibilities on a routine basis. But more importantly, our leaders must reflect on the reason they became an advocate for youth, if they are to successfully affect their kids.

However, I must add that directors have to be careful not to impose their beliefs on leaders, but leave room for their team members to lead in their own individual way. I learned this the hard way when my team Teen Director resigned.

I cannot lie. I was really hard on him. Although it brought out the best in him, looking back, I now see where I thought only of what benefitted the facility and not what was best for my leader as an individual.

In 2013, my Teen Director was leaving, and we threw him a celebration party. Towards the end of the party, he pulled me to the side and said, "I just wanted you to be happy with my ideas versus taking what I presented and stretching it into more." He expressed how he never felt his work was good enough. How I made him feel he had never arrived when it came to my expectations.

This discussion led to a change in the way I work with the leaders who oversee the facilities I manage today. Their ideas may be different than mine, but as long as we accomplish the organization's goals, allowing individuals to lead in their own way, utilizing their superpower is more important.

I learned a lot from that experience. Just like we recommended them to review their "why" on a consistent basis, I needed to go back to what the position entailed. Go back to why we hired the person. Review their strengths that won us over initially. Naturally, we look at people's weaknesses and areas of growth and focus on that too much. I take the Coach Tony Dungy approach now. "Don't tell me about what they do wrong. Tell me what they are great at," and we build on it. Empower a leader's strength.

It is well established that the leader provides the tone for an organization. For example, a decisive leader with a clear vision is more likely to see success than an unorganized and uncertain leader. Leaders who can motivate and inspire those around them are more likely to see their organizations advance.

If Ms. Charles had merely resorted to disciplining my outward behavior instead of pressing to understand my fears when she studied my academic records, I can imagine a different outcome. Young people are particularly impressionable, and their performance can be greatly affected by their leader. If the leader loses hope, a kid's chances of finding it are slim. Our youth need someone who can guide and support their dreams. Champion their aspirations, and help them develop into responsible adults.

CHALLENGE: Re-evaluate why you chose to lead children. Find one kid, if not more, you have experienced a connection with who has that one thing that shows potential, though they may struggle to make the grades. Resist reacting to outward behaviors. Ask questions.

And if you manage leaders, be careful not to force your leadership purpose on them, neglecting their superpower and causing frustration with the job. A burned out, disgruntled leader can become ineffective or even abusive to the kids over time. Those in leadership positions in your organization must be aware of the affect they can have on the young people they serve.

> " *The best youth organizations are not defined by content knowledge… but by skill acquisition through effectiveness and meaningful programs.* "
> *~Kevin A. Brown Sr.*

Your leadership purpose guides your overall leadership style and decision-making.

Can you think back to when you first decided to work with kids, running an after-school location or summer camp program? I refer to the time of innocence when you believed there was no obstacle too significant to overcome in your journey of becoming a confident leader while working with youth. You had a specific reason for wanting to be their leader. I'm sure you had specific goals. You knew what you wanted to accomplish from a passion standpoint.

If you were naïve like me and worked your way up from the bottom, you thought once you obtained a leadership position your students would respect you more and soar to new heights. Maybe you thought parents would take your recommendations for their children and implement your wisdom at home. Did you hope staff would follow your lead and everything else would come easy?

It took me about six months of riding in the metaphorical front seat of a rough roller coaster, and having every one of my assumptions and hopes destroyed, to realize I had a choice to make. I could stay on the same path—to the kids' detriment, and mine. I could end the ride, admit I had made the wrong career choice, and leave the profession. Or I could stop the ride, adjust, and create a new trek according to the facts. Which have you chosen?

Because you are still reading, I am going with the last and believing you are at a turning point, needing to make a decision. I included this section to help you. Say it with me: "Leadership is hard work."

LESSON: Leadership is hard work with the facts, but impossible without them.

Your journey will be more successful if you will get an understanding of all that is required of you at the beginning, know your value and purpose, be in rhythm with life and work, remain faithful to your craft, and be motivated by your passion. Although leadership is complex, it is worth the effort for the youth you serve in your community.

That is why I challenged you to know your "why" and "how." And to revisit your role responsibilities. Your purpose is not something you can simply imitate from someone else, but must become authentic to you and your values. Now, you need to decide which leadership style serves your community best.

I have compiled a few of the positive, and more popular leadership styles various psychologists have identified. (See the toolbox for a list of references):

• **Transformational Leadership**: This style uses inspiration to motivate the kids and team members to reach their full potential. The leader encourages personal growth and development, sets high expectations, and leads by example. Transformational leaders also foster a sense of purpose and passion, creating a positive and empowering environment for youth development.

• **Servant Leadership**: Prioritizes the needs of others and focuses on serving them. The leader actively listens, empathizes, and supports the growth and well-being of their youth.

• **Collaborative Leadership**: Emphasizes teamwork and cooperation. The leader encourages open communication and involvement from all team members, including the youth they are guiding.

• **Democratic Leadership**: Involves the youth in decision-making processes. This leader values the input and ideas of all individuals, allowing them to have a say in matters that affect them. This participative approach not only empowers people but also helps them develop critical thinking and decision-making skills.

• **Authentic Leadership**: Genuine, transparent, and true to their values. This leader leads with integrity, honesty, and consistency, which earns the respect and trust of the youth they mentor. By being authentic, youth development leaders can serve as role models and inspire the youth to embrace their unique qualities and strengths.

• **Coaching Leadership**: Focuses on developing the skills and talents of the people they work with. They provide constructive feedback, guidance, and support, helping individuals identify their strengths and areas for improvement. This leadership style empowers them to take ownership of their growth and development.

• **Visionary Leadership**: This style has a clear and inspiring vision for the future. This leader can articulate a compelling direction and inspire the youth and staff to work toward common goals. By providing a sense of purpose and direction, visionary leaders motivate them to strive for excellence.

CHALLENGE: Depending on the context and the needs of the youth you serve, decide your leadership style or combination of styles you will incorporate. A successful youth development leader can adapt their style to suit different situations while considering what is best for all concerned.

When you are clear about who you are and how you want to show up, it will guide your decisions to stay true to yourself as a leader. Whatever you do, do not let your leadership purpose be compromised by outside forces. Take control of your program and lead it to greatness. You must constantly examine your program's needs, mission, values, and purpose to walk in the integrity it takes to be the phenomenal leader you want to be.

"We often spend more time with the students than the parents do. Parents are trusting us with their kids. What an awesome responsibility!"
~ Keenan Bullard

6

VISION CULTIVATES VICTORY

*L*eaders, your vision matters.

My first professional leadership experience started at the Boys & Girls Clubs of Central Florida, Tupperware Brands Branch in Kissimmee, Florida. Blame it on my college football recruiting days, but I could not be like the coach who sat on the family couch, sold them a dream, signed their child to a scholarship, only for the child to get to the school and receive none of the vision that was pitched to them. That was happening at this facility. For every one child recruited, we lost ten shortly after they got to our facility because the program lacked structure.

I asked my supervisor if we could create a club-wide pedagogical, curriculum including all youth members—a demographic of 56% Latino, 42% Black, and 4% other—knowing it would take funds we did not have to affect the community. I had to tap into a visionary leadership style. That meant coming up with a program, counting the cost, and then funding the initiative. But no way would I ask anyone to do what I was not willing to do first.

In an attempt to bring families closer together, we focused on health factors. I proposed we name our initiative "Go Healthy" and educate both parents and children about living a healthier lifestyle: physically, mentally, emotionally, and spiritually.

The concept called for us to contract a registered dietitian, a chef, and partner with the local Fresh Market stores, among other supporters. Although our objective was to help our members by involving their families, we also made the activity youth led. For the first time ever, we created a community garden. The residents, our students, tended the plot of land, growing fresh fruit and vegetables. They could access the garden even when the facility was closed on Saturdays and Sundays.

The "Go Healthy" initiative included monthly family fitness nights, and registered dietitian nights for parents, a gardening program two days a week, and extended hours we called, "Late Night Basketball."

The Heart of Florida United Way awarded us a small grant to ensure we painted the best picture to significantly impact the community. Donors loved our written proposal. The United Way liked how we involved other entities by hosting well-known guest speakers, and our partnering with Nike, Tupperware Brands Corporation, and Walt Disney World.

LESSON: New to a facility or not, when the team is losing is the moment leaders, aspiring or veterans, are expected to show up and make a play. Early projects like this helped build our credibility when applying for larger grants later, like the $5 million grant I mentioned in the introduction. We will cover those details in the next chapter and Toolbox. When applying for the big bucks, you need a track record of using lesser funds and resources properly, so never despise small beginnings. Every step works together. Give your program time to grow.

When my supervisor granted permission for the "Go Healthy" initiative, he only required me to do one thing—show evidence of the program's effectiveness. I asked my supervisor to give me two years, which is how long I assumed I would need to gather accurate data, conduct a comparison and contrast analysis, and show the overall usefulness. I may have been overselling when I promised to ensure that our after-school program would be the best in the state, but sometimes you have to stick your neck out there and believe big, if things are going to change.

You can have a vision, but the follow-through is what will set you apart as a leader. You do not have to reinvent the wheel, but experiment with the different styles provided in Chapter five and choose what will help you to be most effective.

What can you see your program accomplishing if you choose to take the lead on a possible solution to a problem your facility is facing? Is the leadership style you will need clear? Have you counted the cost to know what and who you need to ask for support? Are youth and staff aligned with your leadership vision?

CHALLENGE: Don't be afraid to offer your ideas. You cannot expect to be the same person next fiscal year as you are now. It is vital that you demonstrate growth. Participate in leadership institutes and conferences and network with other leaders. That way you will be able to slip into the different leadership styles when you must cultivate a victory.

With the new initiative, there could be nine kids already enrolled in the program who are going back and telling their friends, drawing not one but up to ten more kids. Working from the inside out, your vision could be what it takes to turn things around and win at the buzzer. Small wins lead to the big ones.

> *"Building relationships with students and staff is not that complicated. Talk to them. Care about them. Be genuine."*
> ~ *Alkeria Robinson*

The relationships leaders cultivate make living the vision possible.

"I want to see every child safe." Once you understand what *you* want, assess what you will do daily as a leader to make your vision a reality.

Maybe the journey that played out in your head was strong when you first started in the field, but now you lack evidence that you are living it out. Personally, too much of my time spent focusing on discipline issues and high turnover took me off course for a season. However, discovering the importance of positive culture and climate, I had to adjust my leadership approach to include the collaborative style. This leadership style promotes creativity, problem-solving, and a sense of ownership among staff, students, and the community at large to better align with the vision.

At the time, I was working at a facility in Indiantown. The location perimeter did not have any streetlights. We dismissed the kids at 7:15 p.m. From the view outside of my office window, I watched almost three-quarters of the kids walk home in pitch black conditions during fall Day Light Savings season.

The safety issue extended beyond the Boys & Girls Clubs' reach. We could have said, "The governor, mayor, city councilman, and the community at large are responsible for caring for the streets in the area." But a leader does not wait on others to get the answer. He/she is the catalyst, envisioning the problem, and getting results.

How could we get a light at the corner, or help the kids at least get across the street safely? Some fights must go beyond the scope of the job. But we were not sure where to go and how to approach individuals in the area. In that moment, I asked myself, "What would Andrew do?"

Working with him, I got to observe how he built relationships with the very people who managed the city streets. He taught me to be familiar with local politics. Andrew made sure he was in their circles, attending meetings, and taking notes. He believed this kind of leader involvement played an integral part in the development of the child and community.

I can still hear Andrew telling me, "This is who you meet with when you have this problem ..." He taught me what a city manager was and what they do... A councilman or councilwoman. The mayor. State representative.

I wrote a list, made calls, and set appointments with everyone and every entity I thought could help, asking one question. "What does it take to get things done in the city?" I received instruction to write a proposal, go to the city council meeting, and petition for what was required.

No problem. I just had to learn their format. Every city has a slightly different process. It's all about getting immersed in the community.

I secured that information, spoke to the city manager, and then shared it with one of my colleagues who was the director of child prevention. He responded, "'Man, talk to my cousin.'"

I was shocked to learn his cousin was the City Manager. Wanting to be sure, I said the name, and my colleague confirmed.

LESSON: Never underestimate the power of the relationships you have made along the way.

I got all the different leaders to come to the facility where they could see the condition for themselves and hopefully act upon their duty to keep the children safe. I figured most of them were parents first. And what parent would want their child walking in the dark, to possibly be struck down by a driver who could not see the child crossing a street until it was too late.

A couple of months later, they came out for an assessment. The day the city manager, councilmen and women visited the facility, the staff stuck to the schedule and dismissed the kids at 7:15 p.m. The men joined me on the curb, watching the kids leave under the cover of night. As the children crossed the road, I asked the group, "If this was your child, what would you have to say?" Cars sped past, emphasizing the danger. I wouldn't have thought to pray for proof, but took advantage of the moment none-the-less. "So, Mr. City Manager, is this going to be on you?"

Next council meeting, we brought our proposal for a street-light to provide safety for the children in the neighborhood. The vote was unanimous.

I'm not at that center anymore because I relocated to a different organization with the Boys & Girls Clubs organization. However, that experience shifted my mindset to go beyond the inside walls of the facility or what I'm getting paid to do. It also allowed the community to see that what we do as an organization stretches beyond the walls.

CHALLENGE: Be a servant leader, putting the needs of the people first, build trust, and create a nurturing environment where those in your care can thrive. Serve your community.

What is your leadership vision? Is there any evidence you are following it? Have you identified the problem to know how to serve those you are leading?

As a leader of your program and school location(s), it is vital to have a clear vision of where you want your program to go. This vision should be based on the organization's mission, vision, goals, and values that are aligned with your personal beliefs.

"Resiliency might be more important than talent. People who can bounce back from adversity have a huge advantage in life."
- Javian Golphin

Develop a plan to realize your leadership vision.

Having a personal vision with no plans on how to get the results you seek is frustrating. I'm referring to written plans that include S.M.A.R.T goals. These are short-term goals that are **S**pecific, **M**easurable, **A**chievable, **R**elevant, and **T**ime-framed goals, taking you closer to your long-term vision.

I once walked into a facility under my supervision and immediately recognized behaviors flare up among the children. Staff members huddled in a corner as if waiting for someone to come to their rescue. Most were not engaged at all. If the corner had been a door, or even a window, the staff would have escaped.

But when interviewed, these people had proclaimed, "I have a passion for kids." The staff culture of the program was "this is what we do." A complacency to go through the motions and remain ineffective. More fitting, the staff's "I don't *know* what to do" culture had become a norm in their daily operations. Everyone doing just enough to keep from being fired.

It was clear I needed to start from the top and work my way down, re-establishing a semblance of order. There was no structure, no accountability, nobody saying, "no." Leadership had lost sight of our vision to "provide a world-class program experience that assures success is within reach of every young person who enters our doors… demonstrating good character, citizenship, and living a healthy lifestyle."

In this instance, high enrollment handed us the supervision of ninety-four kindergarten and first-graders split between two adult teachers. Even the worst schools don't allow such student-to-teacher ratios. The Club Director had not counted the cost of sacrificing quality for quantity.

The wear and tear on the building would increase repair expenses. God forbid an avoidable accident occurred due to lack of supervision and cost the facility its reputation. That would cost the director his job. The good name of the organization would suffer, and ultimately penalize the parents, kids, and the community, aligning them with the very environment we hoped to save them from.

First order of business for the Membership Coordinator— stop! Put a hold on accepting any more kids. Literally, staff were steadily enrolling more kids while I reviewed the existing student records.

I met with the Club Director to devise a plan so he could realize his initial leadership vision. Back to the drawing board. Literally, we wrote out the plans, brainstorming on a blackboard. We mapped out:

• The script they would use with the parent/guardian to turn away kids. Any who persisted in being granted admission based on the "no limitations" culture that had been created previously were forwarded to me to handle. I did not mind being cussed out.

• How many people are in the building? How many adults, staff, students? Breakdown student count by grade.

• How many adults were needed to balance student/teacher ratios immediately?

You would be amazed at the clarity one receives after writing everything down. At the blackboard there is no casting judgements at others, but everyone works together to solve the problem. It's like spilling the contents of the puzzle pieces onto the table to sort and group the colors and patterns before assembling. The vision. The problem. What you have. What you need. The possible solutions. Timeframes. All are puzzle pieces waiting to be assembled to create the vision.

Calls were made to another colleague at one of the other facilities. His teacher-to-student ratio allowed him to send us two additional teachers to work in our facility for a short time. Yes, a band-aid, but it gave us the time we needed to hire more staff.

For two months, the Club Director and I arrived two hours early every day. We walked that facility, the playground areas, front desk, the parking lot—every corner, every square inch. I needed the leader to take ownership, understanding what he had control over. That way, when he made decisions in the future, he could consider what was best for all involved and all working parts. I truly believe if he had known the limited capacity of his facility, he would not have breached the building code limits, compromising the safety of the people inside.

LESSON: There will be times when the CEO, COO, or your immediate supervisor visit your after-school location and asks for an update. Taking ownership and learning the ins and outs of your program, the people in your care, and the facility will allow you to give insight beyond gym highlights. Knowing the true backstory about everything will show you have full control of your organization's vision entrusted to your leadership. Then your data will reflect it.

Now when I visit the same facility, leadership from the top down, are giving the proper responses they learned from this experience. I asked, "When you tap off at third grade, what do you do?"

The director replied, "Start a waiting list." No hesitation, with his head held high, maintaining contact with my gaze, exuding confidence.

I got excited. To coach a concept is one thing. To see the information received and acted upon is the most rewarding part of what I do. I love to be a part of the growing process with my team. Next, I asked, "What happens when you lose a staff member?"

"Check with my sister organizations. Or sister clubs," he said without any hesitation.

Because the director exuded confidence, his staff was able to do the same. They had what they needed to obtain the results written out and the plans describing the original vision.

Staff no longer huddled in the corners but actively engaged the students. Even college students were brought in to boost the manpower. The program experienced an immediate decrease in behavioral issues among the students that was visible right away.

CHALLENGE: Write out the vision. Develop a plan that includes S.M.A.R.T. goals that will help you and your staff or team. Take steps, even small ones, toward realizing that forecast for your future. Seeing the vision in black & white on paper or screen, takes your commitment to a whole new level. As said in Habakkuk 2:2, "Write the vision; make it plain on tablets, so he may run who read it."

A goal without a plan is just a wish, often leading to disappointment. And a wish is not enough to lead an after-school or entire organization effectively. Otherwise, you will be leading from the sidelines.

What are your short-term and long-term leadership goals to achieve your ideal results? Is your leadership practice important to meet short-term and long-term goals? Can you create a plan of action that supports your leadership goals? Are your goals and plans reviewed regularly? What strategies will you use? What resources will you need to overcome obstacles?

Answering these questions is not easy, but it's essential if you want to be the successful leader you are capable of being.

"People seek leaders who inspire and energize others to do more together than they can individually."
~ Shaige Brissett

BUILD YOUR TEAM WITH GRATITUDE

7

LEADERS LEARN TO LEAD

*S*tudent of Leadership

What is a student of leadership? Someone who actively seeks to understand and develop their leadership skills and knowledge. They study various leadership theories, behaviors, and practices to enhance their ability to lead and influence others effectively.

Does this describe you? Here are a few examples and strategies of my journey of becoming a student of leadership. Hopefully, this will give you a springboard and ideas to begin your own trek:

• **Continuous Learning**: *Engage in reading books, articles, and research papers on leadership. Attend workshops, seminars, and webinars to gain insights from experts in the field.*

In 2019, I completed the Level 2: Advanced Leadership Program (A.L.P.) from the University of Michigan's School of Executive Leadership. This opportunity came because I was enrolled in another continual educational program called

Spillett Leadership University. Sarah Torres, my COO when I was an Executive Club Director at the Boys & Girls Clubs of Martin County, encouraged me to participate. As a result of continually being exposed to various mentors and advanced knowledge, I witnessed production levels increase in the programs I served. Membership enrollment and retention rose 129%. Relationships with community leaders (mayor, city officials, schools, churches, etc.) strengthened. Behavior issues amongst youth decreased by 63%. We completed 100% of grant deliverables, achieved 105% of fundraising goals, and increased parent involvement by 75%. Staff turnover decreased and the list goes on.

• **Self-Reflection**: *Regularly assess your strengths and areas for improvement as a leader. Keep a journal to record your experiences, challenges, and lessons learned.*

As mentioned earlier, I keep a virtual journal where I turn my thoughts into unpublished articles. This is a preferred format to record experiences, challenges, or things I believe need to be addressed and shared one day. Self-reflection, solely by writing, is something I do at least twice a week.

• **Observation**: *Study the leadership styles of successful leaders in various fields. Analyze how they communicate, make decisions, and handle difficult situations.*

In 2020, when I became the Director of Operations at the Boys & Girls Clubs of Palm Beach County, I had the opportunity to witness "greatness" in motion. The COO, Steven Cornette, easily became my standard for success. Viewed from my new position, Mr. Cornette was the Michael Jordan of the organization. He created the acronym I.M.P.A.C.T., Integrity, Mission-Driven, Professionalism, Accountability, Communication, and Teamwork. Mr. Cornette woke up at 4 a.m. His attitude toward hitting targets and reaching all benchmarks had me starting my day two hours earlier to be a similarly impactful player. I gained a new appreciation for what I was doing for the youth and families we served. Now days, it is rare that I do things on impulse, but more with purpose and intentionality— moving from feelings and opinions to facts and data.

• **Mentorship**: *Seek out mentors or role models who can provide guidance and share their leadership experiences. Learning from someone with practical experience can be incredibly valuable.*

Mr. Cornette, Ms. Charles, Andrew and so many more I am sure I have failed to list.

• **Feedback:** *Solicit feedback from peers, colleagues, and team members about your leadership style. Constructive criticism can help you identify areas to refine.*

I ask my staff and colleagues, twice a year to complete 360-feedback assessments on me. Reviewing their feedback is important. This is not to see if I'm liked, but to find out if I need to catch up in my role as one of the leaders in the organization.

I also seek feedback in a more personal way when I take staff out to lunch or dinner. I've learned that people will come if you have free food. Over a meal, we can have a candid conversation on the state of the organization from their point of view. And I get the opportunity to listen to their thoughts. I ask them specific questions about my progress, level of effectiveness, fairness, strengths, weaknesses, and opportunities.

• **Networking**: *Connect with other aspiring leaders and professionals. Engage in discussions, share ideas, and learn from their space.*

I enjoy facilitating and overseeing various community advisory boards. The members usually consist of local leaders, first responders, law enforcement, business owners, military veterans, educators, and politicians. Connecting with these individuals in their respective fields, allows me to strategize with them and see if I am operating most effectively and efficiently. For instance, I recall speaking to law enforcement and city officials about hosting adult basketball leagues at one of our facilities' gyms to help increase the visibility of positive involvement among men in the community. From this conversation, the city decided to partner, and the leagues' men's basketball games have run through the Boys & Girls Clubs facility for the last two years. To see the youth smile when they see their father, uncle, cousin, and brother playing the game is incredible. Receiving praise and recognition from the city manager and members of the commission was an added bonus.

• **Adaptability**: *Be open to adapting your leadership style based on the needs of your team and the situation at hand. Different situations may require different approaches.*

In 2020, during my time as the Director of Operations, I noticed an increase in elderly veteran staff, 85% more than when I was an Executive Club Director. Back then, most staff were younger than me and less experienced. I realized the need to change my leadership approach.

The first 90 days, I refrained from implementing anything new. I asked questions, observed, watching for patterns. I wanted to learn how they operated in various situations. I recall the Teen Center's Assistant Club Director who came into my office and asked, "Mr. Davis, why don't you say anything? We noticed you like to help without taking over a project, take notes, listen when others talk, ask thought-provoking questions, and write on large flip chart paper."

It was nice to see my efforts had not gone unnoticed. I was happy to inform her, "I'm creating a game plan for how we will upset standards and surpass expectations. It will take some time to see who we have on the team (evaluation) and make the necessary adjustments for the betterment of the organization. Hopefully, I'm creating a formula that will last long after I'm gone."

I had to take a strategic approach when communicating, interacting, meeting, delegating, and collaborating with my veteran team. I implemented Sean McVay's, "lead with humility and confidence" approach to get the staff to buy into the system. Head Football Coach for the Los Angeles Rams (at the time of this writing), Coach McVay became the youngest NFL head coach at the age of 30, leading a group of men a few years older than him; even men 10 to 20 years older. Coach McVay and I had a lot in common. Taking a piece from his stellar game plan gave me the hope and inspiration to lead my staff and youth in the community to victory.

• **Empathy**: *Develop strong interpersonal skills and practice active listening. Understanding the needs and perspectives of your team members fosters better communication and collaboration.*

As a family man, I completely understand the importance of one's value system and time. When it came to any of my staff, I had a few non-negotiables I prioritized when evaluating their care or their work:

a. Faith

b. Family

c. Health

d. School

Listing what was priority allowed me to show empathy for the individuals that were in my care.

- **Problem-Solving**: *Sharpen your problem-solving abilities. Leaders often face challenges that require creative and strategic thinking to overcome conflict.*

In 2023, an upset parent sent a disturbing email describing a matter that involved a staff member and her son. The email clearly stated, we had "24 hours" to address the matter before the news and media would be called. This was a situation I knew needed to be solved as soon as possible.

After reading the email several times, I called the parent to get an accurate understanding and to ask questions. The parent was more irritated than the email portrayed. Remaining calm was the only way to effectively deescalate the situation. I earned her trust by exhibiting true attentiveness, and a willingness to resolve her concerns. She agreed to hold off from calling the authorities and media, sharing what had happened.

She claimed staff refused to allow her child to go to the bathroom, causing the student to soil their clothes. Based on the facts given, the Department of Children and Family (DCF) should have been called. Although notifying DCF was the right thing to do, a critical component that stood out during the mother's story caused me to dive deeper into the matter.

It was a race against the clock. The fact that the parent still let her child attend the camp after the incident pushed me to further investigate the matter. I drove over an hour to where the mother's child attended the camp, which was the exact location of the staff involved. After getting three staff witness statements and speaking to five different youth at the facility, it was clear the complaint had been exaggerated.

I arranged a face-to-face with the parents of the youth involved, the staff, their supervisor, and myself. The meeting lasted two hours. It started intensely but ended well. The mother realized that her child had lied about the matter and framed a staff because the child was embarrassed. It was proven that the child only went to the staff member after the accident took place. When the mother realized the truth, she and the father were apologetic, especially toward the staff involved.

In less than 24 hours, after the conclusion of the meeting, the mother sent a follow-up email expressing her appreciation for the supervisor of the staff member and me. She thanked us for professionally handling the matter, loved how we did not isolate her child, and went beyond the call of duty to ensure that every child was always safe.

• **Lead by Example**: *Demonstrate the behaviors and values you expect from your team. Your actions can have a powerful impact on the culture and morale of your organization.*

When I was the Area Director over the Glades facilities, I had seven Club Directors I supervised. It was my responsibility alone to provide the board with updates, growth, and strategic plans for all seven program locations. There was one group of board of directors along with me whose responsibility included fundraising for all the facilities in the Glades area: Belle Glade, Canal Point, Pahokee, and South Bay.

Each of the Club Directors led their own facility: program, youth members, and staff. They complained they did not have a board or any opportunities for their individual gifts, talents, knowledge, and experience to be displayed beyond the scope of their job. However, they all expressed a desire to learn more about leading better in their role.

After a year into my role as the area director and knowing each of the Club director's superpowers and growth areas, I pushed them a little. I had heard all of them, in some capacity, express how they wanted to become an advocate for their facility, youth members, and staff. I decided to do the unthinkable. I arranged for them to present at the next board meeting.

Each Director had to pick a month and present. Instead of me selecting who would present first, their name was entered in a wheel of random name picker. Think, Wheel of Fortune. It started in July so everyone knew who would be presenting at the start and throughout the fiscal year (October 1st-September 30th).

You should have seen the directors when they presented on their assigned month. Man-o-man, they came ready. Some had PowerPoint slides, others had handouts, or showed a video. I was thoroughly impressed, even proud.

To my surprise, the directors indicated they took note of my mannerisms, vocabulary, hidden clues, signals, etc. from watching me deliver information at the monthly board meetings and incorporated these into their own presentations. In this case, the students exceeded their teacher with stellar performances. All the board members were amazed at the quality of work, effort, time, and information that was delivered by my staff.

Each Club Director's confidence and energy level went up. Their performance reviews shot through the roof, and so did their productivity. You could even see it in their staff team.

The Director's level of excitement spilled over into their facilities. They were able to increase their enrollment, handle conflict with little to no assistance from me, strengthen relationships with other organizations, etc. I can rave for days about the Glades Directors.

Many of them are now leading workshops, training, and coaching sessions for the organization. I did what I could to prepare them for the next phase in their personal and professional life. All of us were grinding it out even in the small conference room. They took that preparation and ran with it. Look at them now. They are showing other directors in the organization how to master the art of communication, consistency, and, most of all, confidence.

LESSON: Sometimes we have to get out of the way and let each staff member finally fly like the eagles God called them to be.

• **Delegation**: *Learn to delegate tasks effectively, empowering team members while ensuring tasks are completed efficiently.*

We conduct our annual Step Show in Belle Glade, Florida, every year. This is where over 100 youth in grades K-12 perform and display their gifts and talents through stepping, cheering, and dancing. A lot goes into making this one-day even happen. With almost 1000 people packed into a gymnasium, I must ensure all preliminary factors are in order long before the event day.

Planning starts in late January, after our annual golf fundraiser. We have three pre-event meetings. At these meetings, we discuss ticket prices, concession stand food items, marketing, staff assignments ... And I could go on.

We split into teams, dividing and conquering the many tasks. To save time explaining everything, I typically handle the larger items such as fundraising, board of directors, purchasing and ticket prices. While the rest of the team executes their task(s), we can all see no one person bigger than the brand. Everything is for the betterment of the youth in the community.

Being one of the leaders in the organization, I still love to roll up my sleeves and get into the trenches with the Clubs and staff. To see how the entire vision come to fruition is beyond amazing. Every year gets better and better. Not to mention that the fundraiser goal increases, and every year, we meet our target.

In the end, the kids, parents, and community leaders are happy with the results we put into creating such an energetic, powerful, and remarkable event.

CHALLENGE: Become a student of leadership. It is a continuous journey. Actively seek opportunities to learn, grow, and refine your skills to become a more effective and impactful leader.

What will you do to extend your leadership knowledge? Where will you go to gain the information? How long are you willing to take? Who will you seek to mentor you?

In my case, as I stated earlier, I followed the advice of a mentor to further my education and deepen my leadership knowledge by enrolling in an advanced leadership program. I knew I needed to sit at the feet of someone, a professor who could give me the proper tools, strategies, concepts, methods, and techniques. The rewards I experienced from the program have been endless.

"It is not about one person. It takes a team to accomplish anything."

~ Shatavia Warren

Performance Review: Are staff more competent because You lead them?

Early on in my career, Henry Saxon, a great man who became my mentor, once told me, "The purpose for your supervision of staff is the continual improvement of leadership." These words have stuck with me for a long time. I used this phrase often to gauge my effectiveness and concluded, if those under my leadership are not seeing an increase in their performance review scores, clear communication, goal setting, and ongoing professional development is needed. This required me to become a student of leadership.

Some studies have shown that the leader's competence impacts the follower's perception of their own ability. In other words, when leaders are seen as competent, their staff also see themselves as competent. This is known as the "halo effect" and can significantly impact a team's performance.

As a student of leadership, I can admit that I have failed numerous times. But the wisdom I have gained from both failure and success is priceless. Since, I believe there is no joy in possession without sharing, I choose to do so now. Let's examine a running list of lessons I gained along the journey of becoming a confident leader who leads other after-school program professionals.

LESSONS:

• Clearly communicate your organization's performance criteria and expectations for the role they are being hired to do. Better yet, considering the performance review process should be a two-way conversation, provide the youth development leader with a blank copy at orientation. This will make sure they are aware of the specific goals, objectives, and competencies they will be evaluated on. Also, it allows time for them to ask questions.

• Ask leaders to conduct self-assessments of their performance based on the established criteria. This encourages self-awareness and helps leaders identify areas for improvement.

• Schedule regular one-on-one meetings to discuss progress, challenges, and achievements. Have a deep dive session to go over the vision and offer guidance and support, ensuring your leaders are on track to meet their goals.

• Offer relevant training, workshops, and resources to enhance leadership and professional skills. This could include communication skills, conflict resolution, team management, and youth development best practices.

• Encourage leaders to keep track of their accomplishments, projects, and positive outcomes. This documentation will be useful during the performance review to provide evidence of their contributions and your effectiveness in leading them.

• Create an environment where feedback is actively encouraged. Regularly seek input from colleagues, peers, and the youth they work with. Constructive feedback can help leaders identify blind spots and areas for growth.

• Help leaders identify and address any challenges they are facing without taking over. Provide guidance and support to overcome obstacles that may hinder their performance.

• Constructively address areas where improvement is needed. Offer specific feedback and suggest actionable steps for growth. Work together to create a performance improvement plan that outlines steps for addressing those challenges.

• Recognize instances where the leader has collaborated effectively with other team members, departments, or community partners to achieve shared goals. Emphasize how they have demonstrated strong leadership skills, including communication, team building, mentoring, and problem-solving. Emphasize the positive impact the leader has had on the youth they work with.

• Discuss the leader's future goals within the organization. This could include opportunities for advancement, further training, or new responsibilities.

• Collaboratively set S.M.A.R.T. goals with your youth development leaders. These goals should align with the organization's mission and the leader's responsibilities.

Do you make your team more effective because you are leading them? Is it your leadership that motivates your staff? How can you help your staff be more effective? How do you help your leaders to grow professionally each year? What professional development resources are you providing your staff members? At what point in their development do you care about their growth and learning process?

CHALLENGE: Be a student of leadership. Start by fostering open communication, setting clear expectations, and providing ongoing support, so you can help your leaders excel in their roles and achieve positive outcomes for the youth they serve. Remember, their performance review scores are a reflection of your leadership.

Although other factors also play a role, your leadership certainly impacts the team's overall competence. (See Toolbox for a sample of the Performance Review.)

"Adults tend to focus on tasks and projects and forget the basic principles we learned in kindergarten, such as being respectful and playing nicely with others."
- Candace Burrs

8

GREATNESS IS UPON YOU

$\mathcal{T}$he Interview

I recently completed an interview, asking me about the infamous **$5 Million Dollar Grant.** I decided sharing that question-and-answer session here with you, my fellow leaders, a great way to wrap things up.

Question #1

How did it all start? What was your mindset going into applying for the grant?

Answer:

A grant is much more than free money.

It answers all things. It is every lesson and challenge made in this book. It is a culmination of hard work, years of failures as well as successes, relationships developed, and teamwork, showcasing the strengths of many different people who were willing to be challenged.

Most people may not know that public schools must fundraise for their necessities. All that the school budget doesn't cover is dependent upon fundraising. Like new bleachers. That's not a budget item. So, a culture of, "How can we help the school out as well as meet our needs," became my first order of business. Especially, considering the type of grant we were pursuing.

The 21st Century grant is a federal grant that any entity with an educational component can apply. Our thinking had to become one with the core focus area of the Boys & Girls Clubs of America's, academic success.

Traditionally, kids come into our programs with homework. We strive to get them to whatever mastery level we possibly can. It's a different ballgame when you go from thinking how to get the funds to cover your facilities' needs to seeing things from a prospective of, "how can we collaborate even more with the school to help one another?" But know this, knocking on school doors is not easy. Especially, when you're an outside entity trying to come in. Think, Fort Knox, because they have different red tape. But securing our kids' future is worth the struggle.

Also, schools see themselves as the true hub to meeting the student's needs academically. So, you want to come in and do certain things, but typically, the answer to all that is, money. Our mindset embodied the question—What are you bringing to the table?

Question #2

How did you learn about the grant?

Answer:

I learned about it from another after-school program I worked at. I knew we needed to organize focus groups, pull a team together, and discover how to connect with members of academic standpoints. That had been the key to the other facilities' successes, so re-inventing the wheel was not an option. We adopted what had worked for them.

Question #3

You keep saying, "we", "our". Who were the team members you chose to work with? Please, list your answer.

Answer:

You can only be as great as your team. There are so many working parts, before and after receiving a grant. No one person can effectively meet the demands to produce the promised results at this magnitude. I cannot encourage sharpening your people skills enough, starting with personal development. Here is a detailed list of the committee who helped write the grant:

• CEO

• COO/Chief of Staff

• VP of Finance/Chief Accounting

• VP of Operations

• Chief Grants, Strategy & Compliance Officer

- Club Director/Executive Director

- Education Director

- Board of Directors & Advisory Board Members

- Local school Principals

- Parents of the students

- Students

- Program Director

- Assistant Club Director

Question #4

How did you get them to work together, forsaking their egos with so many leaders in their own unique fields working on the project?

Answer:

Focus groups!

When you have senior leadership, you must challenge their unique strengths. I drilled them with questions. They had to know what we were working for was much greater than ourselves. Vision unites people. And when a leader vividly portrays the vision with consistency, confident leaders answer the call, denying themselves to gain the results they seek.

Inside those first meetings, we brainstormed. Communicating the vision is so important. Find a way to reach your people. We used diagrams, wrote the vision on the board, used Post its. I don't know how many, but we built a fantasy-vision board. We got the analytics. Collected data from the districts to tell us what the kids in our community were missing. We had to figure out the gaps—math standpoint and reading. We didn't have time to get caught up in egos, or think of ourselves, for thinking of them.

Then, we continued to go back to our mission. I plied them with questions, asking, "What are we doing? Why are you here? What is the true need? We know what we want, but which one of you will do what it takes to make an impact? Why? Is it only good enough for students to just graduate high school or do we really want to ensure that they have a plan for the future as well?"

Everyone had to answer the questions. We had seven to eight different focus groups, pulling back the layers of the why. Why *we* needed the grant?

Question #5

That's a lot of WHY questions? Redundant even. And it seems you spent a large amount of time planning. Why?

Answer:

I understood the responsibility that came with obtaining a grant that size. Once you get the money, you're on the hook. You must produce. There is no more going back. You are locked in.

The focus groups had to be so detailed, pulling back layer after layer of the why, until we got to the core of how we were going to do it in real time. Then built up to the reason why we needed the funds. It's not about five million. We could've gotten ten million.

I put the five million on the board and asked, "what would you do with this?" A person in the room was chose to share what they would spend the money on. What they would not buy.

Putting the information on the board helped them to see what five million looks like and how they would use the money. I'm a visual person. I had them to draw their center, draw their community, draw the school, draw the kids, the books, and picture in it in life.

Then I broke the focus groups into designated groups—administration, literature-based standpoint, to keep us up to speed for the deliverables. Meeting certain benchmarks, criteria, and maintaining it is detailed work. It's hard.

Another group represent the people in the programs—groups versus individuals.

Then the groups assimilated into departments, which is how we developed the team for this grant. It wasn't going to come from one person. This was going to be an effort because of our vision being grand.

I'm talking about a landscape of approximately 14,000 kids. You know, so again, that's the reason why we had so many focus groups. The responsibility that came with the grant was going to be a beast. I had to get the team to believe that we could beat the beast. That it could be done, before the trials came.

Question #6

You mentioned you also had to sell the vision to the school principals in your area? Why?

Answer:

To be awarded the grant, we had to obtain written consent from the principals. If the school already had the 21st Century grant we could not be within a three-mile radius. Which means the state would have been like, "the kids you want to serve, send them to the school."

For us, that meant speaking to eight schools at this particular location, eight different principles. Including, four or five different community chairs we have to impress.

Question #7

How did you come up with the spiel?

Answer:

This is my job. I learned early; you have to hop in with the educational field lingo. That requires calling the district. I contacted friends I know and telling them I need data.

I requested data on the schools in the three-mile area with neighborhoods that qualified for the grant. A portion of the grant, you will need the average medium income in the area. There is school data to indicate if they are a title one school— 80 to 85% of its students on free or reduced lunch. Certain percentages have to be at or below poverty line to qualify.

By the time I spoke to the committees, I had gathered the hard data. I had the school's literacy rate. The math rate, I got the high school rate of regulation and proficiency.

Our goal is to go into the meetings and sell them on how we can help them to improve based off the programs we already own. Beyond playing basketball after school, many would be surprised to learn that the Boys & Girls Clubs of America organization average:

•99% of its members graduate high school.

•Reductions in the school's pregnancy rates, dropout rates, and prevention rates that include mental health. We actually have online data, but it's hard to pinpoint what we do that causes this overall effect.

Question #8

What is one thing, you are most proud about, the Boys & Girls Clubs have spent the money on that the schools in the area probably wouldn't have been able to do for the students?

Answer:

One thing I'm incredibly proud the Boys & Girls Club spent the money on, which the schools in the area might have yet to be able to do, is the establishment of our after-school art program. With the grant funds, we were able to provide a dedicated space for creative expression, art supplies, and professional art instructors. This program has given youth in our community the opportunity to explore their artistic talents and develop their creativity in a way that might not have been possible within the constraints of a regular school budget.

Question #9

If you had the grant application process to do all over again, what would you do differently? Why? Why not?

Answer:

If I could redo the grant application process, there are a few things I would approach differently:

1. I would invest more time in researching and understanding the specific requirements and preferences of the grant provider. This would help tailor our proposal more effectively.

2. I would involve a more diverse group of individuals in the application process to bring different perspectives and insights.

3. I would consult with other organizations similar to ours to weigh the pros and cons. This would give us a projection of possible challenges that we may face and come up with a robust game plan.

I believe these changes would make us more thorough and effective in our approach to receiving the grant as we endure all the opportunities that come with it.

Question #10

What lesson have you learned? What was yours or the team's biggest challenge?

Answer:

Since receiving the grant, the most important lesson I've learned is the power of collaboration. Our biggest challenge was realizing we could only achieve our goals in collaboration.

We needed to work closely with other organizations, schools, and local businesses to maximize the impact of our project. Learning to navigate and coordinate with various stakeholders was a valuable experience, and it taught me that achieving meaningful change often requires a collective effort. This lesson in collaboration has been both rewarding and challenging, as it demands effective communication and teamwork, but it ultimately leads to more sustainable and significant results.

CONCLUSION

LET'S WRAP IT UP!

~

When it comes down to it, trying to find quick solutions and formulas for running an after-school care program is like resorting to diet pills or beauty products to improve one's health. They don't work.

There are no short cuts! Especially when what we do affects our children, our future leaders.

It's a challenge to learn skills and the how-tos for developing a functioning management system while not neglecting the human side of your program. But being the difference in a child's life and their future makes the hard work rewarding.

Although many resources can help you accomplish this end, I'm honored you've chosen *You be the Difference: Challenging After-School Program Professionals to Lead with Confidence* to serve as a source to help navigate you back to your foundational love for youth development.

Like you, other directors are going to seminars and conferences all over the country to improve their work. Although this may seem like a quick search for ideas, a more profound need often brings them together. It is okay to want and create a safe place to release the burdens we carry. Just remember, before you can help the children, the process begins with self-care.

In my experience directorships of early childhood programs are often sought by people who want to make a positive difference in the lives and well-being of families. Many directors face the reality of the situation and are conscious of the "if only" feelings that linger below each breath. If only they had more money to pay staff, improve the facility, reduce regulations and paperwork, offer more scholarships, get more parents involved, and make this work more meaningful.

Many people seek employment in youth development agencies or non-profit organizations because they are not only looking for a steady income but also because it has real meaning and the potential to make a difference by touching and healing the hearts of people. However, too often, we lose sight of our original motivations after external pressures, and the demands that this work requires us to meet, overshadows them. Sometimes the original goals we had for our job may fade away or seem impossible to achieve. Our minds and hearts quickly become overwhelmed by the workload, staff, program structure and quality, budgets, regulations, reports, and parents who are often unhappy. It is difficult to find the time to go to the toilet, let alone get through all the reading and paperwork needed. I can empathize with you when having to move from crisis to crisis, too exhausted to remember the time-management strategies and too frazzled.

In the end, I can only hope that you found a quote, strategy, or story that was enlightening and assisted you in regaining a sense of new possibilities. The purpose of *You be the Difference: Challenging After-School Program Professionals to Lead with Confidence* was to elevate YOU, your mindset, improve how you deal with obstacles, opportunities, and bring awareness to the forefront so you can no longer suppress the elements that will springboard you to greater heights. I pray you no longer neglect how you envision and do your work. I encourage you to embrace the newness that comes along your journey as a youth development professional (leader). Yes, this journey can seem difficult and the destination distant, but you only need one step to get there.

Great leaders are committed to being the difference. Being a true change agent. To take your professional skills to the next level, you must practice and develop emotional intelligence and self-awareness. Youth development leaders should live by the words, "When you learn better, you do better," and continue to improve their leadership skills.

As a leader, your growth is never finished. You must position yourself to engage in experiences that empower you to lead and transform. Find opportunities to develop your leadership skills. Get out of your comfort zone and learn from others. Think of the level of training athletes undergo to prepare for athletic performances. Only an athlete can be successful if they have the mindset of a champion, so they train like champions.

Train hard for every skill that you're working on. The journey to excellence is not finished. Although the journey is never ending, the stops along the way, when you can celebrate your wins and achievements, are priceless. You will find another way to travel if you take the time to reflect on your journey.

Take all your knowledge and experience with you as you gear up for another adventure. When the journey gets difficult, and as long as you have breath in your body, you will always have an opportunity to pursue and achieve excellence!

With the help of this book, I am confident that your journey will be easier. Don't forget the little things along the way—the everyday impact you have on every child and their family, your staff and colleagues, and the community you serve. Your leadership can have an impact on the lives of others and make a real difference. I'm talking about the real things that money cannot buy.

Although your purpose in this field requires a lot from you, I am confident that you can handle it. How do I know? Because there's nothing regretful when you have a heart of a servant leader. One who accepts the challenge to be the difference and lead with confidence. Remember, **"Confident leaders are built ... not born."**

"Every community has an unsung hero... whether you want to believe it or not, it's you."
~ Anthony J. Davis Sr.

9

LEADERSHIP TOOL BOX

*S*ports Illustrated magazine cover of Deion Sanders link:

https://sicovers.com/featured/october-9-1995-sports-illustrated-october-09-1995-sports-illustrated-cover.html

Book List

Here are the books:

John Maxwell

The 360 Degree Leader: Developing Your Influence from Anywhere in the Organization

Steve Gruene and Todd Whitaker

Committing to the Culture: How Leaders Can Create and Sustain Positive Schools

. . .

Napoleon Hill

Think and Grow Rich

Brian Tracy

Management (The Brian Tracy Success Library)

Jim McCormick

The First-Time Manager

Quint Studer

The Busy Leader's Handbook

Gino Wickman

Traction: Get a Grip on Your Business

Raymon Kethledge and Michael Erwin

Lead Yourself First: Inspiring Leadership Through Solitude

Lonnie Pacelli

Why Don't They Follow Me? 12 Easy Lessons to Boost Your Leadership Skills

Shanda K. Miller

From Supervisor to Super Leader: How to Break Free from Stress and Build a Thriving Team That Get Results

Mary Abbajay

Managing Up: How to Move Up, Win at Work, and Succeed with Any Type of Boss

Jon Gordon

The Energy Bus: 10 Rules to Fuel Your Life, Work, and Team with Positive Energy

Paul Falcone

The First-Time Manager: Leading Through Crisis

Sample Daily Routine

SAMPLE DAILY ROUTINE

5:40 am: Spiritual development

6:00 am: Create and send daily inspiration and encouragement message to staff.

6:30 am: Go for a morning run or workout to clear your mind (mental and health).

7:30 am: Shower and get ready for work.

9:15 am: Arrive at your work location or Administration Office.

9:20 am: Facility walk-through (safety measures).

9:40 am: Check and reply to emails. Do your best to keep all emails under ten.

11:00 am: Text or facilitate virtual or in-person meetings (general

overview and game plan with the operations team).

12:00 pm: Go to another work location (if something is

pressing or for support) ... this gives you time to return calls

(concerned parents, community partners/leaders, school principals,

organization CEO, COO, or direct reports, etc).

. . .

12:30 pm: Arrive at the after-school location and conduct a safety walk-thru (starting with the parking lot).

12:45 pm: Address any or all issues with your staff (provide feedback and coaching).

1:00 pm: Get a bite to eat and send a reminder text to all direct reports to ensure they follow all safety protocols.

2:00 pm: Members (kids) arrive at the facility from school (Greet them at the door. Provide in-person support).

2:00 pm - 6:00 pm: Be on the floor ensuring the safety and Operations at program locations.

6:15 pm: Check and reply to all emails.

6:45 pm: Meet with direct reports and staff (feedback and coaching).

7:00 pm: Interact with youth (basketball, football, teen talk, career exploration, cards, pool, SAT prep, homework help, etc.)

7:45 pm: Closing procedure with the facility leadership team

8:15 pm: Lock up with the team and ensure staff get to their car safely. If anyone is waiting for a ride, wait with them until they are picked up. This can allow time for a deeper conversation with staff to gain insight on how you can improve

as an organization as well as learn more about the staff.

8:30 pm: End your work day.

*On Friday nights, I drive three and a half hours to my in-law's house to be with my wife and children. I am with them for the weekend. I leave on Monday mornings around 5:30 am to make the three-and-a-half-hour drive to work, and my day starts at 9:15 am.

CONTACT FOR ALL COACHING/SPEAKING NEEDS:

Anthony J. Davis, Sr.

Founder/CEO

Absolutely Determined, LLC.

E: Absolutelydetermined2@gmail.com

W: https://www.absolutelydetermined.com

PERFORMANCE REVIEW FORM

EXAMPLE

Performance Review Form

Name:
Date:
Date of Hire:
Location/Title:
Review Type: **90 DAY REVIEW**
This form must be returned to the Human Resources Manager by the end of the month.

Check the appropriate box.

INSTRUCTIONS: This appraisal form must be completed by the immediate supervisor based on performance standards previously established. If the overall is BELOW STANDARDS, the supervisor must contact Human Resources for assistance prior to meeting with the employee	EXCEEDS STANDARDS	ACHIEVES STANDARDS – PROFICIENT	ACHIEVES STANDARDS	BELOW STANDARDS
JOB KNOWLEDGE				
QUALITY OF WORK				
PRODUCTIVITY				
DEPENDABILITY				
ATTENDANCE				
RELATIONS WITH OTHERS				
COMMITMENT TO SAFETY				
SUPERVISORY ABILITY (applicable only to designated supervisor positions)				
OVERALL APPRAISAL RATING (one CATEGORY must BE CHECKED)				

EXTRA! EXTRA!

Ever the instructor, please allow me to leave you with statements I feel will benefit you during your reflection time, on a rough day:

• The heart of why you came to youth development (early childhood) is ...

• Keep in mind your vision and what it could look like.

• You can create an organizational culture and systems that support your dreams.

• You desire to do meaningful work that makes an impact on the world.

• Joy and laughter are the best ways to keep you inspired and push you past the challenging days.

• List areas where you can make genuine connections with others outside of your usual work location.

• A community where you feel safe, have history, and enjoy a sense of belonging.

This reflection time can help you create a vision that guides the direction of your work.

"Leadership is about creating a sense of urgency to rise above the status quo … and empowering others to join you in the journey."
~ Brandon Battle

I urge you to keep improving your leadership skills as you continue to grow in your journey in youth development. It all starts with self-examination. Being a leader requires understanding your superpowers, growth areas, and emotions. Knowing your strengths and weaknesses allows you to determine which skills are most important to the program's success. Nobody has all the skills to run an after-school program on their own. It takes effort, humility, and time. You can build on your strengths and find ways to improve your communication skills, forge meaningful relationships, make financial decisions, and any other skills you may need.

Your beliefs and motivations can be a mirror, giving insight into your emotions. This is another important ingredient in effective leadership. You might be prone to refusing to accept help. Or you may not want to confront people when necessary. These blind spots can impact your relationships with others and your ability to get things done. It is easy to let your emotions cloud the situation when interacting with someone at work or with family. If this happens, take some time to learn why.

You will be able to recognize and distinguish your emotions from the situation, and you will be able to see different perspectives. This will allow you to work in a team and produce a solution. Your staff will be able to see you as a supporter and guide by providing guidance.

Are your staff protected under your leadership?

Productivity is a great indicator of burn out. Or if your staff is like mine, they make a point of voicing their feelings, saying things like, "Mr. Davis you are a good man and all, but I am tired." Being that the staff I currently serve, are much older, they usually feel free to give me a piece of their mind.

When focusing on performance, you cannot overlook the emotional health of your leaders and how it affects their work. According to Education Week, "nearly three-fourths of teachers are experiencing frequent job-related stress. Fifty-nine percent of teachers say they're burned out." Job-related stress and burnout are factors that can limit effectiveness and lead to untimely turnovers. And as you well know, the needs of most after school programs, especially post Covid, cause our leaders to operate as the administrator, teacher, coach, parent, and counselor. I would imagine the stress levels and burn out percentages among our leaders are even higher.

Because this is a topic I hold dear, sharing how I protect the eight, now twelve, Club Directors under my care for this section seems the best fit. If it were possible, I would do the same for all the staff, but I realize my limitations. My hope is that the Club Directors and other staff will duplicate my concerns and protect those under their care, a domino effect until all staff members are covered.

The first component is to develop a relationship with leadership that goes beyond the superficial. I took the first year with the staff to study how they operated. I'm a key indicator type of guy. People telegraph stuff. Please bear with the sports talk, but that is where I learned the concept and transferred it into my leadership style with my staff.

Again, identifying what someone telegraphs about themselves is very important. That means realizing their actions, their productivity, and the way they generally operate. Noting their inconsistencies. Note when there is an increase in their use of sick time or doctor's appointments. Are they working, but their attention to details gradually becomes lackluster? Are they arriving late and leaving early. The complaints, usually non-existent, grow in frequency.

I documented when it generally happened and marked my calendar. Especially near the time they would be biting at the bit to take a vacation. Then, I would usually call and say, "I want you to take the next three days off. Call me back in an hour with your decision."

"What? I don't know what to do," was the popular response. "I have so much to do." Their reactions generally included every reason why they should not take me up on my offer. But it has never failed to date, they call me back within the hour to say, "I'm so glad you told me that," and they accept.

I reassure them not to worry about anything, and I personally go to their facility, stand in as host, and cover their duties for the three days. Staff was instructed not to call their directors for any reason. Problems arise, we would figure things out on our own. It was up to us to make things happen.

Another component I used to protect them was learning their love language. Use the toolbox to see my list of favorite books. This required me getting to know their families, going to their personal events to meet parents and other close relative to glean such information. Not only are my staff older, but they mostly reside and were born and raised in the same community as the facility. But I mainly share this with you, to retell a lesson I learned.

Gift giving is one of the five love languages. Once I learned what the staff liked, I made sure my Christmas gifts during Secret Santa events, anniversaries, birthdays, were thought out well enough to let them know how much I care about them, personally beyond the work they do.

Make sure the gifts run along the lines of candy, books, coffee, gift cards, things like that. No flowers, perfume, or personal items that could give someone the wrong understanding.

"There is no substitute for authenticity. You have to genuinely care about the people in your organization."
- Jame'Keria Sneed

Identify Your Leadership Traits

Your personal beliefs and values influence how you lead the program and what your organization stands for. Integrating your professional voice and personal principles will give you the power, passion, and authority to lead others. You can identify your values and beliefs by looking at mentors and leaders in your life that have either inspired you or disappointed you. What are the qualities you admire most in leaders? What are your worst qualities?

These questions will help you to think about your leadership style and how you approach professional relationships.

•Are you more organized and detail-oriented than a big-picture person?

•Are you more outgoing than reserved?

•Am I more likely to work with others collaboratively or authoritatively? What situations am I more likely to behave in each manner? Why?

•Do I emphasize completing the task or finding the best way? What does the situation say about how it changes?

•How comfortable do I feel with conflict and disequilibrium? How can I manage situations that involve them?

•Are you flexible? If not, how can I be more flexible? But am I too flexible if that is the case?

•Is my communication style more direct or indirect?

•Am I quick and easy to make decisions or slow and deliberate?

•Are my feelings private or public?

•Am I more inclined to try new approaches or stick with the tried-and-true methods?

These qualities can profoundly impact your relationships with family members, staff, and children.

Your leadership style has a direct impact on how you interact with staff members, families, and other participants in the program. There are many leadership styles that you can choose from, but I recommend being effective in any style. Choose a process that shares the responsibility and power to achieve an organization's goals. This involves forming partnerships with staff and giving them more control over issues that impact them daily, like resource allocation, curriculum, and scheduling. By allowing families to voice their opinions on policies and daily experiences, you will be able to continue building meaningful relationships with them. Inspire and encourage group participation by actively inviting community leaders to share their ideas and perspectives on improving center processes. Encourage individuals to use their strengths and encourage engagement. However, some decisions are ultimately within the director's control, such as budgetary or hiring staff. An effective leader will seek input from family members and staff before deciding. An influential director who adapts to every situation, regardless of their tendency to lead in one way or another, will be a good leader.

Book a consult @ www.absolutelydetermined.com if you need more information.

> *"Don't just listen to people who make you feel good or make you feel comfortable. Listen to people who challenge you. They can make you better both personally and professionally."*
> *~ Jada Davis*

Find a Better Rhythm

Effective directorship requires skillfully balancing competing demands to maintain a successful early childhood education program. I want to provide you with seven principles that will guide your work and life as you get into a better rhythm with how you operate personally and professionally.

• **Time Management (Return on Investment)**: Set realistic, short-term, and long-term goals for both personal and professional purposes. These goals should be written down and reviewed regularly. If necessary, they can be adjusted. To avoid procrastination, you can establish a priority order and time limits for each task, regardless of your daily, quarterly, annual, or annual to-do list. Time is not a barrier or limitation. You gain experience as you go along and reap the rewards of the observations, reflections, and relationships you have built.

- **Learn to let go**: You got this job because you can do many things well. Perhaps you are a perfectionist willing to put in extra time or days to improve the report, update the welcome board, or plan for staff meetings. However, a one-size-fits-all mentality can prove detrimental in a situation with multiple demands. It is essential to distinguish between expectations and needs. These are often different, and your expectations may be higher than what you actually need. It is important for you to recognize when you have done enough. Instead of wasting time trying to make it perfect, move on. As with many other things, this is where you can be a role model to your staff and fellow colleagues. You have the chance to model moderation.

A second skill that is essential for an effective, confident leader is the ability to recognize that you cannot do it all yourself. You must recognize when it is okay to say no and when it's time to delegate. Although declining a request from a teacher or parent can be difficult, you should not feel disappointed. You and your program should permit yourself to say no when you cannot take on more. Recognize the strengths of your staff and share responsibility with them. Sharing your talents with your staff is often more efficient and productive.

- **Exercise "Rotated Neglect"**: You have to ensure that all aspects of your job are focused while acknowledging that something will be neglected. You cannot do it all at once. I found that rotating neglect was good practice as a director. This means you put some tasks on hold, and give your attention to others. It also helps to keep track of the progress of other tasks, switching them out when necessary. You can achieve balance if you don't neglect the same project every day, week, or month. You can set small, achievable goals within the more significant, longer-term scope of larger, more complex undertakings. Identify what you can do today and what you will do tomorrow.

• **Take some time for yourself**: Being a director, manager, coordinator, or whatever your official title or role, means caring for others, including children, families, staff members, board members, community members, and other program constituents. Because you are bogged down with taking care of others and making sure they have everything they need, the only thing you tend to neglect is yourself. You should include self-care in your daily routine. This could be exercising, taking a walk, reading a book, meeting up with friends for lunch, or getting out of your office. It would benefit you greatly if you made it a priority to find time for yourself before you tackle your work. You don't have to make time for work if you want to go to the gym or take a 5-minute music break. However, it is vital to balance work and your personal well-being. You can take better care of yourself and others when you do.

• **Be a lifelong learner**: Even the best professionals understand that learning and growth are ongoing. It is essential to support your staff's professional growth, but you also need to support your own. It is essential to continue learning by pursuing your interests and keeping up to date on research, best practices, and tools in early childhood. Here are some ways to be more effective and engaged as a lifelong learner.

1. Subscribe to digital or print journals. You can visit other early-childhood programs to observe them and invite teachers and leaders from other early-childhood programs to visit yours. This is an excellent opportunity to share your ideas and get feedback.

2. Take continuing education courses at local colleges and universities (in-person or virtually).

3. Visit other local programs.

• **Support Groups**: Directorship can be lonely. You are often so busy running your center to the point where you don't reach out to other colleagues in similar positions. Networking is a great way to get support, share tips and solutions, and find help. Begin small and meet up monthly with a few program leaders from your local area to exchange ideas. These directors or like-minded individuals could be people you know or have met at conferences, local grocery stores, social media, and church. Or they could be someone you contacted via email to local program location to set up a meet-up. You can either organize your own director's support group or hire a facilitator. Director groups can be formed by local community organizations such as early childhood councils or childcare resources.

• **Be an intentional decision-maker**: While you may not always have all the resources that you require or desire, you have a vision, goals, power, and the ability to make decisions that will move your program forward. You are responsible for the outcome of your decisions regarding curriculum, budgeting, and hiring staff. You must be strategic and understand the reasons behind what, why, when, and how. When you are so ingrained in the details of your day, it is easy to lose sight of the bigger picture. It will make your decisions and actions more meaningful if you take a step back from the details and pause to look at the bigger picture.

"The synergy that results between passionate and supportive parents and community leaders is ridiculously awesome. It is what drives great programs and deepens the overall impact on our youth; it builds a thriving community,"
- Kirk Patrick

Don't Hide. Just Seek.

I hope that you will also stop focusing on the skinny mirror or any other equivalent crutch and instead find ways to feel comfortable in your skin. Vulnerable grace allows you to be your best, no matter how good your hair is or how unsure of your clothes. We are more likely to hide our true selves and make it difficult for others to see us. These conversations build the soft skills needed to guide others through difficult waters.

• **Ask for feedback**. Ask someone who isn't directly involved to observe you and then share their observations. Learn from the feedback you receive. Pay attention to the details and not the person providing your assessment.

• **Keep a record of yourself**. If possible, record yourself in a staff meeting. You can also record yourself practicing what to say in difficult conversations. You can then review the recordings and identify facial tactics or inflections in your voice. Then, tweak your delivery and share it with others in real-time. You can stop focusing on what you see in the mirror.

• **Eliminate the mirror**. We often make assumptions about how others view us. Don't be self-deprecating or doubt your ideas and dreams because others may not like them. Have you found yourself discounting, or unable to share your vision in fear that others will downplay? The fear is real. Writing this book took so long, because of the fear and doubt, but I found it to be liberating to fulfill this lifelong dream. Not because it's perfect, but because I hope to inspire others that there is nothing we cannot do. Do not let your story of who you are and what others think about you drown out the truth.

Keep it 100: Be Real with Yourself

Be straightforward: You must be authentic and vulnerable and keep practicing soft skills to improve your relationships. Empathy and openness to the opinions of others allow you to learn and grow in any setting. Be compassionate no matter the circumstance.

• **Be you.** No matter what program space area you enter, makeup or without, in a suit or sweatpants, be authentically you. Consistency builds the trust it takes to earn the respect of others. This doesn't mean that you can change the outlook on your students or staff. But you can be an influence.

• **Be a person first and a title last.** Especially, when making difficult decisions that can impact relationships. After a difficult conversation, be sensitive to the other person, but careful not hide behind a title as cause to isolate yourself. The message you are conveying risks being lost if you walk away or avoid the other person. By doing so you're making the conversation personal and not professional. In the people business, it is essential to remove layers of thick skin. To improve the relationship and show empathy go out of you may have to go out of your way to serve the other person first. Leaders go beyond the title and practice small, genuine kindnesses, to improve their relationships.

• **Avoid awkward silence.** As a confident leader, you are expected to move first, even if it seems awkward, while practicing empathy. Don't wait for the other person to come to your aid, even though you may want to. Start small talk, then go to the person, smile, wave, and begin a conversation. A script may be helpful if you are in a difficult situation.

"Staff members might respect the position and respect the title … but loyalty is inspired and earned by the leader."
~ Renard Bennett

ABOUT THE AUTHOR

Anthony J. Davis Sr. is an international speaker, certified executive coach, and youth development leader who values dedication, service, and excellence. As a decorated nonprofit executive, Anthony brings unique perspectives gained from his personal and professional experience to empower educational institutions and youth development organizations to unleash the untapped potential of their students, which will benefit the community.

As a former high school All-American (football and track), Anthony humbly participated in the TRIO program at Palm Beach State College (PBSC). The life-changing strategies he learned in TRIO propelled him to become a first-generation college graduate and the national male NCAA scholar-athlete of the year (football) at the University of Central Florida (UCF).

Since 2008, Anthony has dedicated his life to making a difference in the lives of youth and families in underserved communities by being a voice for them in corporate board rooms, courtrooms, and classrooms. As the Senior Regional Director of Operations at the Boys & Girls Clubs of Palm Beach County, Anthony manages the operations of 11 after-school program facilities and is responsible for the lives of over 13,000 K-12 students and 450 employees.

Outside of working for the Boys & Girls Clubs, Anthony is a highly sought-after speaker, executive leadership coach, and professional development trainer. He is known for his leadership, passion, innovation, and creative thinking in problem-solving; he has shown how to motivate and inspire students to upset standards and surpass expectations. As an advocate to shift the mindset and behavior of youth, staff/teachers, and parents, Anthony has proved his talent and reached milestones no matter where he is planted.

As a man of faith, Anthony knows that he cannot do anything without God and the support of his family: Ericka Davis, his wife of fourteen years, and their four children: Zoriyah, Zaria, Anthony Jr., and Amarii.